D1730426

ODES OF KLOPSTOCK.

ODES OF KLOPSTOCK

FROM 1747 TO 1780

TRANSLATED FROM THE GERMAN

BY

WILLIAM NIND

FELLOW OF ST. PETER'S COLLEGE, CAMBRIDGE, AND AUTHOR OF
THE "ORATORY," ETC.

LONDON
WILLIAM PICKERING
MACMILLAN, BARCLAY, AND MACMILLAN, CAMBRIDGE

1848.

LONDON:
GEORGE BARCLAY, Castle Street, Leicester Square.

TABLE OF CONTENTS.

TRANSLATOR'S PREFACE.

"IF for some years past," says an Italian critic,
"the enthusiastic admiration of the 'Messiah' has
considerably declined,—if the defects of that poem
are now more severely criticised, time has only
served to increase the lyric reputation of Klopstock,
who will always be regarded as the PINDAR of
Germany."

"No one," says the German critic Gervinus,
"had attained to the true tone of bardic inspiration,
to the simple sublimity of Hebrew poetry, and to
the genuine spirit of classical antiquity, in the same
degree as Klopstock in his earlier Odes ; where we
seem to listen in turn to Horace, to David, and,
what is more extraordinary, to Ossian, before the
world knew any thing about him.   Such gifts were
not possessed by even Lessing and Wieland.   They
first rekindled in Herder, but only to imitation, and
afterwards in Göthe to original production.   .   .   .

" One class of his Odes is spiritual, another bardic, and a third classical : the first, hymnal and dithy-rambic ; the second, artistic in form but involved and obscure in substance ; the last, simple and sustained. The first has relation to the MESSIAS, to David, and, the Prophets ; the second, to the tone of the Edda and of Ossian ; and the third, to Pindar and Horace. These last, which are formed upon the classical model, are incontestably the best."

The translations now offered to the public comprise, with a few exceptions, the Odes which were written in the best period of Klopstock's poetic life — from his twenty-third to his fifty-sixth year. A few brief biographical notices will be a necessary introduction to them.

He was born of respectable parents in 1724, at Quedlinburg, in Prussia. At an early age he shewed much strength and hardihood of character. Among the healthy sports which he prosecuted with zeal *skating* had a prominent place, and he has celebrated " Tialf's Art" in more than one ode.[1] In his

[1] The enthusiasm with which the *boy* GÖTHE committed Klopstock's hexameters to memory, and the care with which he afterwards wrote out his early Odes (because "welcome and dear was all that came from him"), appears from his " Passages of my Life "— *Aus meinem Leben.* But the reader may be amused to learn the practical effect which these Odes on Skating had upon that extra

boyhood he is represented by his friend Cramer as a young Cheruscan hero, such as he afterwards sang

ordinary man. " This joyous exercise," he says, " we owed also to Klopstock. I well remember springing out of bed one clear, frosty morning, and declaiming to myself (' *Schon von dem Gefühle*,' &c.)—

> ' Already with the glow of health elate,
>   Descending swift the frozen shore along,
>   The crystal I have whiten'd with my skate,
>   In mazes as to Braga's song.'

My lingering and doubtful resolution was at once decided. I flew forthwith to the spot where so late a beginner could discreetly practise his first attempts. And in truth this exertion of strength well merited Klopstock's commendation. It brings us in contact with the freshness of childhood, calls the youth to the full enjoyment of his suppleness and activity, and is fitted to avert a stagnating old age. Hence we followed this sport immoderately. We were not satisfied with thus spending upon the ice a glorious day of sunshine, but we continued our motion late into the night. For while other modes of exertion weary the body, this seems constantly to lend it new strength. The full moon emerging from the clouds over the white meadows frozen into fields of ice, the night air whistling to our onward motion, the solemn thunder of the ice falling in upon the receding water, the strange distinct echoes of our own movements, brought before us Ossianic scenes in all their perfection. Now one friend, and now another, sounded out in half-singing declamation one of Klopstock's Odes; and when we found ourselves together in the dim light, we were loud in sincere praises of the author of our joys.

> ' For should he not immortal live,
>   Whose art can health and joy enhance,
>   Such as no mettled steed can give,
>   Such, e'en, as pants not in the dance ?' "

in his Bardicts. About his sixteenth year his poetic
genius was developed, and he began already to medi-
tate some great epic poem, which should elevate
his country to a rivalry with other nations, whom it
had hitherto distantly admired. He seems, like
Milton, to have turned his first thoughts towards
some ancient national subject; and the Emperor
Henry the First, commonly called Henry the Fowler,
engaged his attention. Two or three odes still bear
witness to this early predilection. But subsequently,
upon his entering on a course of theology at Jena in
his twenty-first year, his mind settled upon a Christ-
ian subject—the MESSIAH. The rude habits of
Jena little according with his disposition, he soon
removed to Leipsic, where he formed a circle of most
intimate and congenial friends. He lived with his
distant relative, Carl Schmidt, for whom he enter-
tained the warmest affection; and soon became
acquainted with Cramer, Ebert, Gärtner, Giesekè,
Gellert, and others, whom he celebrates in his early
Odes with that enthusiastic ardour of friendship
which was so *german* to his nature. He welcomes
them to the bardic Elysium, "WINGOLF," and con-
fers on each his appropriate award of praise.

To this circle of friends he communicated the
first cantos of his "MESSIAH," which, meeting with

their warm applause, were published in 1748. Many
of his Odes bear witness to the religious spirit in
which this great poem was undertaken and prose-
cuted.   Whatever difference of opinion there may
be as to its merits, either in a religious or a poetic
point of view, it is evident that Klopstock wrote it
in a spirit of deep devotion, as a sacrifice of praise to
the Redeemer.   No poem ever produced more ex-
traordinary and lasting effects.   It was received with
incredible enthusiasm in all the states of Germany,
and opened a new era of national literature.   It
called forth the genius of Germany, gave it confi-
dence in its own impulses, broke the bonds of slavish
imitation, and dissipated the depressing *prestige* of
foreign superiority.   The Odes speedily followed in
support of the same cause; and thenceforth the
German Muse started on a new course, in fair com-
petition with the British, with no small disdain of
the French, and fearing none but the Greek.   Even
this fear, at a later period, Klopstock bade his coun-
trymen discard ; and in " The Hill and the Grove"
he prefers the warmth and genuineness of Nature, as
it is found in bardic poetry, to the fascinations of
Grecian Art.

    In his earlier years, friendship was to him in the
place of love, and little inferior to it in intensity.

"More than mine eye can tell thee, loved my heart," is his language to his friend Carl Schmidt; and on more than one occasion we are reminded by the warmth of his expressions of the lament of the sweet Singer of Israel over his friend Jonathan. "I am distressed for thee, my brother Jonathan : very pleasant hast thou been unto me : thy love to me was wonderful, passing the love of women!"

But love, in its ordinary sense, marked the next stage of our author's existence. He formed an attachment, such as might have been expected from his ardent temperament, to Schmidt's sister FANNY, whose name finds place in many an exalted ode. She is said to have been clever and fascinating, and capable of appreciating his genius; but she was insensible to his addresses, and perseveringly and finally rejected his hand. This disappointment cast him into a state of profound melancholy, which gives a sombre tinge to some of the most remarkable of his Odes. At one moment his grief finds strong and energetic expression, and at the next beguiles itself with the loftiness of his imagination. He took pleasure at this time in indulging in a morbid, but very poetic, sentimentalism. The English reader will probably also be struck with the extraordinary juxtaposition and blending of ideas earthly and heavenly, which is characteristic of Klopstock's mind; because the earthly was pure and the heavenly poetical.

He was roused from this state of depression by a visit to the Swiss poet BODMER. The Swiss received him with little less veneration than would have been due to an inspired prophet. The scenery by which he was surrounded (witness the ode entitled "The Lake of Zurich"), and the patriotic feelings which he seems to have imbibed in the land of mountains, gave a turn to his thoughts; and as he recovered the cheerful joyousness which was natural to him, the sympathising ladies of Zurich were surprised and staggered at the metamorphosis. His poems made them weep; but the poet did not.

That wise and Christian prince, Frederic V. of Denmark, whose consolation it was at the close of life, in an unsettled age, that he had never shed a drop of blood nor wronged one of his subjects, was so much delighted with Klopstock's religious epic, that he invited him, at this time, to Copenhagen, and settled upon him a pension to enable him to devote himself to the completion of his poem. Frederic and his consort Louisa (daughter of our George II.) are duly celebrated by our bard, though he was no praiser of princes. Much later he felt himself bound to vindicate these encomiastic strains, when an excess of patriotic indignation led him to write an ode against " Prince-praise," which I have thought it just to render into English, though it is scarcely translatable from its undignified bombast. The reader will not confound Frederic V. of Denmark with his contemporary Frederic the Great. The former is Klopstock's admiration, the latter his aversion. The selfish ambition of the Prussian Frederic, his love of war, his contempt of every thing German, and his devotion to French literature and infidelity, stripped him, in Klopstock's eyes, of every claim to admiration, and even to decent respect. Not for a moment is he dazzled by the exploits of the great hero of the age.

On his way to Denmark he had formed an acquaintance with a very amiable and gentle-spirited lady,—Margaretha, or Meta, Möller, the daughter of a respectable Hamburg merchant. The result was a correspondence and confidential intimacy between them, which in four years ripened into a devoted affection, and in 1754 he came to Hamburg and married her. She is the Cidli or CISLY of the Odes, and to her belong all those stanzas (such as the " Rose-wreath," " Her Slumber," &c.) which have any connexion with amatory subjects subsequently to his rejection by FANNY. The transition

is marked by the ode entitled "The Trans-
formed."

His marriage with this lady was very felicitous.
He was at the height of his reputation abroad, and
he found affection and gentleness in his own home.
But in four years' time it pleased God to remove his
beloved partner by death. In 1771 he left Copen-
hagen and settled permanently at Hamburg. His
chief works, in addition to his Odes and the "Mes-
siah," were "Spiritual Songs," many of which were
intended for purposes of congregational psalmody;
"Dramas," partly sacred and partly national; "Gram-
matical Dialogues;" and his "Republic of the
Learned," greatly esteemed by Göthe. He lived
to see his country take that position in literature
to which he had opened the way; and the men of
high genius who were now filling Europe with their
fame, looked up to him with deference and venera-
tion, as the patriarch of their Augustan age.

He died in 1803, when he was on the point of
entering upon his 80th year; and was attended to
the grave by the authorities, foreign ministers, and
an immense concourse of people from the two cities
of Hamburg and Antona. A copy of his "MES-
SIAH" was laid upon his coffin when it was deposited
by the side of his affectionate Meta, in the little

village of Ottensen. They sang over his grave his
favourite hymn, " Auferstehen, ja, auferstehen, wirst
du," &c. of which a translation is given at the end
of the volume.

His Odes, as the reader has seen from the
criticism of Gervinus, may be divided into three
classes,—the Classic, the Hebraic, and the Bardic.
It is in the last that the obscurity, which is generally
charged against him, is most painfully felt.   When
his friends complained to him of the difficulty of his
language, he proudly replied that " they could learn
it."   But a translator must take humbler ground,
and endeavour to mitigate obscurity.   This may
partly be done in the translation itself, since pe-
culiarities in our language do not necessarily involve
peculiarities in another; but remote allusions and a
cloudy dimness of outline cannot, through any
medium of translation, be daguerreotyped into per-
spicuity.   Here the chief resource is in notes and
explanations.

It is thought that it would be convenient to give,
at one view, so much of the Eddaic, or Scandinavian,
mythology as is necessary to explain the Bardic
allusions of these Odes.

In the place of the Deities of Olympus we have

ODIN (or Woden), the Father of all the Gods, and
his wife FRIGGA, who is probably the same as
HERTHA (the Earth); of whose worship Tacitus
gives a particular account. Apollo and the Muses
are represented by BRAGA, the god of poetry, with
his Telyn, or Harp; and his wife, IDUNA, who is the
keeper of the apples of immortality, without which
the gods would grow old and infirm. Instead of
Parnassus and the Castalian Fountain, we have the
sacred Oak Groves and MIMER'S SPRING, which
imparts wisdom and poetic inspiration. THOR is the
Thunderer; and ULLER (for *ice* enters largely into
the northern mythology) is the patron of skating.
The Graces are represented by NOSSA, or HNOSSA,
daughter of the goddess FREYA. LOBNA and WARA
(Love and Troth) preside over lovers. HLYNA is
the goddess of benignity and kindness; and GNA is
FRIGGA's messenger.

The Elysian Fields are replaced by the Oak
Groves and the temples of WALHALLA and WINGOLF
—the former ODIN's HALL, or the Hall of Heroes;
and the latter the temple of Friendship: but the
words are often used synonymously. To these
abodes the warriors who fall in battle, and, ac-
cording to Klopstock, the Bards, are called by the

VALKYRES, or choosers of the slain, who are also
their attendants. They hand to them their drinking-
horns of ale or mead, when they return from their
daily battles, in which they hew each other in pieces
for pastime, and then repair unharmed to the feast of
heroes.   The three Destinies, called NORNS, are
WURDI, WERANDI, and SKULDA (the Past, the
Present, and the Future).   SKULDA bears a wand,
and WURDI a destructive dagger.

Those who are not worthy to enter WALHALLA
are consigned to the dreary abode of HELA (Death),
where their condition is rather one of discomfort
than of positive punishment.

Much reference is made to TUISCO and his son
MANA, or MANNUS, the mythological ancestors of
the Germans.

The OAK, the LAUREL, and the PALM, are fre-
quently alluded to, as the symbols respectively of the
Teutonic, the Grecian, and the Hebrew Poetry ; but
when the last is not in question the PALM also
denotes the Greek.

The principle of translation here adopted must
be left to the judgment of the reader, but the cha-
racter of the versification calls for a few remarks.

Klopstock is the avowed advocate of the cause of ancient rhythm, as opposed to modern rhyme. He devotes an ode — which I have left untranslated — to the celebration of the Spondee, the Dactyl, the Choreus, the Creticus, the Choriamb, the Anapæst, the Bacchœus, and the Pæon. Not only does he freely adopt the Horatian forms, but he is a liberal inventor of novel and elaborate measures, constructed on similar rhythmical principles. And he expresses some contempt (though he has elsewhere used them in sacred verse) for the "jingling sound of like endings." Facilities were afforded for this freedom by the genius of his native tongue — a language abounding in prepositive and inflexional syllables, and sounding all its terminal vowels; though I believe he is thought by his fellow-countrymen to have carried his rhythmical theories to excess; and Göthe, while acknowledging his genius and power, recommends the young poet not to take him as a model. But whatever may be the case with the German, in a language like our own — with few inflexions, overburdened with consonants, retarded by heavy monosyllables, and making a dumb show of a tithe of its vowels — such measures are peculiarly intractable. Many of them, if attempted, instead of being smooth as "Uller's dance upon the crystal sea," would be a dance among the rocks. So alien are they to the vocal genius of our tongue, that, I imagine, no success of execution would make them appear to the English reader any thing more than an exercise of ingenuity.

I have therefore avoided all imitation of the classical and similar metres, and have availed myself of the assistance of rhyme, with which, I think, a language of slow movement cannot, in lyric measures, advantageously dispense.

With regard to the religious opinions of Klopstock, I would not, as an English Churchman, exactly vouch for every shade of sentiment which I translate. It is a satisfaction, however, to deal with an author who, in the whole tenor of his writings, employed so nobly and worthily the high gifts which he possessed. Of no poet of his age could it be more justly said that,

> " He wrote
> No line which, dying, he would wish to blot."

The general tendency of all his Odes is to promote humanity, friendship, patriotism, and religion. Nor ought it to be forgotten, that at a time when an eclectic scepticism was supposed to be the badge of Genius and Philosophy—when the tide of Infidelity was billowing up Europe—he planted the CROSS above the waves, and sang to his fellow-countrymen GOD, THE REDEEMER.

May 1848.

THE DISCIPLE OF THE GREEKS.

HE on whose birth the smile of Genius fell
    With bright and consecrating spell ;
Whose boyish form Anacreon's fabled dove
    Flutter'd disportively above,
And gently closed his wrapt Mæonian[1] sense
    To scholiasts' noisy dissonance,
And lent him wings to soar with free delight.
    Shading those wrinkled brows from sight—
He hears not when the victor calls, enwreathed
    With bays on which a people breathed
Their withering curse, when on the iron plain
    The wailing mother sought in vain,

[1] Homeric.

O'er the last kiss and bosom-rending moan,
  To snatch her bleeding, dying son
From thy stern grasp, O hundred-arméd Death,
  Unpitiful of pleading breath !
If e'en with kings be cast his destined life,—
  Strange to the clang of battle-strife,
And looking down with deep and shuddering dread,
  Upon the dumb-extended dead,
The soul he blesses that has reached the shore
  Where slaughtering hero slays no more.
The lavish praise, the tale immortal told
  Of wasted honour, leaves him cold :
Cold, the expectant fool whose wondering gaze
  Commends him to his friend's amaze ;
And cold, mere Beauty's smile, devoid of mark,
  To whom our Singer[2] is too dark.
Yearnings of better fame did they inherit,
  Who live for ever :—they whose merit,

---

[2] Elizabeth Singer is intended ;—a German lady who married
our poet Rowe, and wrote, amongst other things, " Letters from
the Dead to the Living." Having often prayed to God that her
death might be sudden, her desire was accordingly fulfilled.

Still flowing down as swollen rivers run,

　　Fills up the ages one by one.

Such yearnings lead him to those pleasant streams

　　The proud but thirsted for in dreams !

And if that rarer bliss he haply find —

　　A sensitive and sister-mind,

The tear he calls forth with his scallop shell

　　Is pledge of tears that deeper dwell !

WINGOLF.[1]

First Lay.

As GNA[2] impetuous, on a youthful wing,
And proud as if to me IDUNA's gold
The Gods had reached, the friendly band I sing,
　　And greet with bardic harp-tones bold.

Lov'st thou, O Song, the measured minstrelsy?
Or wild as Ossian's harp that spurned control,
Or Uller's[3] dance upon the crystal sea,
　　Leap'st freely from the poet's soul?

---

[1] WINGOLF, in the mythology of our northern ancestors, was the temple of friendship in the Bardic Elysium. It is often used as synonymous with WALHALLA.

[2] GNA was the messenger of the principal goddess, FREYA; and IDUNA kept in a golden cup the apples of immortality.

[3] ULLER is distinguished from other gods by his beauty, his arrows, and his skates.

The Hebrus rolled with eagle-speed along
The Orphean lyre, that erst the forests bowed
Until they followed the enchanting song,
    And the rocks staggered from their cloud.

So flowed the Hebrus down ; and with it bore
That shade-appeasing head replete with blood,
Still following in death the lyre before,
    Tost high upon the whirling flood.

So flowed the wood-stream downward to the main !
So flows my song in torrent strong and deep,
Scorning the soul that hears the soaring strain,
    And with the critic loves to creep.

Greet him, my lyre, with glad and festive lays,
Whom from afar the beckoning Valkyres[4] call
To pass the lofty threshold, crowned with bays—
    The threshold into Wingolf's hall.

---

[4] VALKYRES, goddesses commissioned to call the spirits of
heroes to Walhalla, and to minister to them.

Thy bard awaits thee.   Fav'rite of soft Hlyn,[5]
Where was thy dwelling ?   Com'st thou from the rills
Of Hæmus and the fountains of the Nine ?

    Or from the eternal Seven Hills,

Where Flaccus' song, and Tully's glowing page,
Did rev'rently the ear of Scipios[6] claim ?
Where with the Capitol the Mantuan sage

    Contended for immortal fame,

And on the enduring marble proudly cast
His thought secure : " A ruin thou shalt nod,
Be dust, and then the playmate of the blast,

    Thou and thy thunder-bearing God ?"

Or haply wert thou borne from Albion's coast ?
O EBERT, love the island of the brave :[7]
They too are German, and the sires they boast

    Came boldly o'er the billowing wave.

---

    [5] HLYN, the goddess of friendship.

    [6] SCIPIOS, *i.e.* good judges, such as Scipio was.

    [7] The *root* of this compliment to my fellow-countrymen is transplanted from the next stanza, " *Lieb von Britanniens* STOLZEM *eiland.*"

So be thou welcome! ever welcome still.
Where'er thy birthland, fav'rite of soft Illyn!
From Tiber dear, dear from the Thracian hill,
    Dear from Britannia's isle of green.

But dearer when thou breathest of the hills
Of Fatherland, from where the bardic throng
With Braga[8] sings, and where the Telyn[9] thrills
    To touches of Teutonic song.

Yea! and thou comest! EBERT, thou hast quaffed
The spirit-fountain of the silver stream![10]
Already the intoxicating draught
    Doth wildly in thy bright eyes gleam.

" Whither, O Bard, does thy enchantment call?
What drank — what see I?   Buildest thou again
Tanfana?[11] or (as once the Theban wall
    Amphion[12]) the Walhalla's Fane?"

---

[8] BRAGA, or BRAGOR, the god of poetry. IDUNA was his wife.

[9] TELYN, the lyre of the bards.

[10] That is, of MIMER, the fountain of poesy and wisdom.

[11] TANFANA, a national temple of the ancient Germans.

[12] That is, by the power of song, as Amphion is said to have drawn the stones to their places in the walls of Thebes.

All the spring-floor my GENIUS has spread bright,
And hither calls our friends ; that face to face
Reposing here in Wingolf's halls of light
　　With wings of joy we may embrace.

Second Lay.

They come !　IDUNA in the rhythmic dance
Goes before CRAMER with the lyre upborne ;
Before him goes, but throws a backward glance.
　　As on the wood-top looks the Morn.

Sing yet those strains of Eloquence,[13] that wake
The swan in Glasor as he floats along ;
His wing he sets, and his slow-bending neck
　　Curbs to the music of the song.

When sings our Fatherland in after years
The war-notes of her bards (whose Bards we are !)
Thine will she sing amid the clash of spears
　　When she goes proudly to the war.

[13] One of Cramer's Odes is intituled " Spiritual Eloquence."
GLASOR is a grove in Walhalla, whose trees have golden
branches.

The spirit of the battle-god is sped :
But while the corpse rolls bloody down the Rhine.
It lingers on the shore among the dead

   And listens o'er the Land of Vine

But thou art silent, and thy tears are seen !
Why died the lovely RADIKIN [14] so soon ?
Fair as the flush of morning, and serene

   As night beneath the summer moon.

Take these fair roses, GIESEKÈ ! to-day
Velleda water'd them with gentle tears,
While feelingly she sang to me the lay,

   That told thy love-mate's griefs and fears.

Thou smilest ! Ah ! that tender-beaming eye
Subdued my heart long since unto thine own.
When, at the first, I looked upon thee nigh,

   And saw thee, but was all unknown.

When I am dead, my friend, so sing of me.
My parting spirit at the tender lay
Shall feel thy tears' attraction, true to thee,

   And while thou weepest, lingering stay.

[14] Cramer's Bride.

Then my good angel, silent and unknown,
Shall three times bless thee ; circle thrice thy head ;
Three times look after me when I am gone ;
    Then be thine angel-guard instead.

Hater of Folly, but man's friend sincere,
Right-hearted RABNER, full of honest glee,
Thy cordial, open countenance, is dear
    To friends of Virtue and of thee.

But terrible thou art to Folly's brood !
E'en in thy silence scare them from thy path,
Nor let the cringing smile that apes the good
    Conciliate thine indignant wrath.

Prostrate and proud — they are no more transform'd !
Make thy soul tranquil ! E'en though as the sand
They multiplied — though all around them swarm'd
    Philosophers throughout the land,

If one thou dost reclaim from every age
To sit with those who come at Wisdom's call.
Well done ! and we will sing thee, mighty sage,
    And wait for thee in Wingolf's Hall.

Winking my grandchild, I will set thy bust
By Tibur's satirist, and Houymess' friend ;[15]
And thou shalt bear a noble name — THE JUST !
    To which not many can pretend.

Third Lay.

More gently sound, my lay, more softly flow,
As on the roses from Aurora's hand
Drop the light dews : for, see ! with cloudless brow,
    My GELLERT greets the festive band.

The loveliest mother's loveliest daughter dear
Shall read thee, and look lovelier for the bliss ;
And if she find thee sleeping, will draw near,
    And bless thee with an innocent kiss.

One day, beside me, resting on my arm,
The friend whose love in all my love has part,
Shall tell me the sweet tale in all its charm,
    And teach it with a mother's heart

[15] Horace and Swift.

To little Zilia.   None like thee can draw
Virtue so worthy of the public scene.
When those two noble maidens first I saw,
  In magnanimity serene,

(Mere beauty could not imitate the deed)
Entwining their bright hair with simple flowers.
Mine eye bespoke my heart's o'erchargèd need,
  And rained itself in silent showers.

A deep and serious joy that day was mine.
O Virtue, cried I, thou art fair to see!
How is the soul a masterpiece divine
  That elevates itself to thee!

Come, OLDÈ, for thou lovest us, come near!
Clear-sighted, fiery soul, that canst not brook
Pretentious smatterers;—to all severe,
  Prate they of Virtue, or THE BOOK.

Thou, who wert sceptic, then philosopher,
Derider next of all that men regard,
Then Milton's, Homer's, high interpreter,
  Then misanthrope, then friend, then bard,

Thou hast lived ages, KÜHNERT, ere thy prime !
Ages of iron, silver, and of gold !
Turn back, my friend ! back to the bard sublime,
    And to Mæonides of old !

Two more I see.   One hath our ancestry
And fonder friendship bound in mutual vow ;
And one, the charm of sweet society,
    Pure taste, and the exalted brow.

SCHMIDT is what I am : and the Valkyres bright
Call us together to the sacred grove :
And ROTHÈ yearn'd for Wisdom's freer light,
    And lived to Friendship and to Love.

Fourth Lay.

Ye still are absent, friends of future years !
Where dwell ye ?   Speed, O Time, thy wingèd race,
And wheel round the bright hours, ye circling spheres,
    When I shall see them and embrace.

Thou, my belov'd, that shalt be mine alone,
Where dost thou linger ? for with yearning sight
I seek thee in the far and dim unknown,
    And through the labyrinths of night.

If still of tender hearts the tenderest
Stays thee, impetuous, with a mother's hand,
Well is thee ! thou wilt learn upon her breast
    Virtue and love to understand.

Already has the Spring her rosebud wreaths
Strewn in thy path, thou restest in her shade ;
Virtue and love the air around thee breathes,
    And tears thy gentle eyes invade.

The moisten'd eye with tender feeling fraught,
(Which shew'd me thy whole spirit at a glance—
Its bright serene, the far flight of its thought,
    More light and fair than western dance)

The mien of goodness, and of noble grace,
The heaving heart that thrills to feelings fine,
The thought that it will give me *there* a place,—
    The lovely phantom all is mine.

Thou, thou art absent ! Lone and woe-begone
I wander, seeking thee through many a tear ;
Thee, my belov'd, who shalt be mine alone,

 And love me,—but thou art not near !

Fifth Lay.

Saw'st thou the tears that from my heart o'erflowed,
My EBERT? Sad, and leaning on thee now,
Sing me,[16] inspired, some serious British ode,

 That I may feel as glad as thou.

Ha ! all at once my kindled eye is bright,
Bright is my countenance, and bright my soul.
I see far off beneath the dimmer light,—

 I see far off in Wingolf's hall

The holy shadows slowly pass along !
Not those that rise so sadly o'er the dead ;
But such as waver in the hour of Song

 And Friendship round the Poet's head.

[16] " He read English poetry to us with much animation."

The wings of inspiration bear them nigh,
Plain e'en to eyes no genius filled with light;
Well may'st *thou* see them, spirit-beaming eye,
    That piercest with the Poet's sight!

Three shades approach! The air about resounds,
As when the springs of Mimer hear above
The oak-wood's rushing roar, and Wisdom's sounds
    The listening Echoes learn and love :

Or when, to Braga's harp, on yonder height,
From the rock-altar of the Druid throng,
Down the deep valley of the forest-fight
    Is hurled the wild and lawless song.

Thou, who dost wander grave, yet glad the while,
With eyes of peace, and lips of pleasantry,
Who art thou? See, he turns on me a smile!
    Yes, 'tis our GÄRTNER—it is he![17]

[17] I have compressed two stanzas into one by omitting an
obscure parenthesis which alludes to some of Gärtner's works.

Dear to us as Quintilius was of yore
To Flaccus, friend of naked truth and light,
Gärtner, return ! return for evermore !

　　But ah ! thou fleest from our sight.

Oh stay, my Gärtner, stay ! Thou could'st not go,
When on that sad and melancholy eve
We gather'd round thee in our silent woe,

　　Embrac'd thee, and took mournful leave.

Those parting hours, that evening, shall be kept
For ever in memorial sad and true.
There first I learnt, while in their grief I wept,

　　How nobly lov'd the noble few.

Our midnights shall be many in the grave.
Ye that come after, give those hallow'd hours
To genial Friendship, as your fathers gave :

　　The pattern of your age is ours.

Sixth Lay.

Beaming intelligence, his arm in mine,
Sang Ebert,—" Hail thee ! EVAN HAGEDORN !
Yonder he steps forth from the bowers of vine,
    Stout-hearted as the god Jove-born

" My bosom glows !   The joys my senses quaff
Through all my trembling frame tumultuous roll.
Spare me, Lyæus,[18] with thine ivy'd staff,
    And with thy juice-o'erflowing bowl !

" Him a young Bacchante — not of Orpheus' foes —
In youth with vine-leaves featly cover'd o'er ;
And he became a marvel to all those
    Who drank the waters that did pour

[18] Evan and Lyæus were names of Bacchus.

" Into the valleys down the rocks, and sate
By springs to which no vines their shadow gave.
So slept he, careless of their loud debate,

    Not without gods, an infant brave.[19]

" Thee too, Apollo, with his garland crown'd :
Laurels, inwove with myrtle, o'er thee nod.
As arrows from the golden quiver, sound

    Thy lays ; as arrows of the god

" Ringing behind him loudly as he ran.
Chasing the flying Daphne through the wood :
And oft, as laughter of derisive Pan

    Ere the woods echoed to the mood.

[19]   " Non sine Diis animosus infans."

    " Nicht ohne Götter ein Kühner Jüngling."

(The poet seems to allude pleasantly to the " marvel," that
Hagedorn should be a minstrel of the vine among a water-
drinking people ; for he was born at Hamburg, far from the
vine-country.)

" To wine and song fools think thee destin'd still.
Because to the unwise, the thoughts that most
Stir in the noble an exalted will,

     Fade in the distance and are lost.

" Thy heart beats manly ! and thy life sounds more
Harmonious than an unforgotten lay.
Thou, in an age that shuns Socratic lore,

     To a few friends dost lead the way."

Seventh Lay.

So sang he.   In the dimness of the grove,
Of Wingolf's grove far off, I saw among
The sacred oak-shades, deeply musing, rove

     SCHLEGEL,[20] contemplative of song.

[20] Johann Adolph Schlegel.

Sound ! and to him the sounds poetic came,
That quickly shaped themselves to words that burn.
For he had pour'd into his lay the flame
    Of genius from the sacred urn.

One thing is wanting ! knit thy critic brows,
That, if that golden age shall e'er be ours,
Dull spirits may not in the shade repose,
    Nor swarm about Tuisco's bowers.

Eighth Lay.

Come, Golden Time, that dost so rarely dwell
With mortal men ! come at our prayer, and bring
Airs of the shady grove, and sounds that swell
    Melodious from the silver spring.

Nature breathes round thee, lost in rapt delight
And lofty musings !   Dearly she enfolds
The souls that feel their strength, and dare the flight
    That solitary Genius holds.

Nature ! I heard thee thro' the infinite
Move, as when Argo[21] with the harmony
Of spheres, by poets heard in the still night,
    Sails brightly through th' ethereal sea !

Through all the golden ages thou wert dear
To hallow'd bards : to bards of elder time,—
Bards of the latter world, who see thee near,
    And bless thy holy form sublime.

[21] One of the most beautiful of the constellations.

TO GIESEKÈ.

Go ! and I will tear me from thee, though to sorrow's swollen lids
        Manly virtue naught forbids.
Go ! my friend, I will not weep thee : grief would deluge all my years
        If for thee flow'd down my tears.
For they all like thee must go ; and, fleeing, each the other leave
        Sadly, lonely, here to grieve.
So death severs wife and husband : he afar has found his grave
        Gurgling down the ocean wave.
She on shore, where bones upcast and shiver'd wrecks and storm-tost sand
        Pile her tomb upon the strand.
So the bones of Milton slumber far remote from Homer's bones.
        And the solemn cypress moans
O'er the one in dismal wailings, that are wasted ere they come
        Sighing o'er the other's tomb.

So has God inscrib'd in heaven silently on tabled brass
        All that here shall come to pass.
What was written by the Eternal low in dust I read with awe,
        Nor with tears would blot His law.
Go. beloved ! other friends perchance embrace thee, true and dear,
        Friends that shed no parting tear,
Unless tears bedew their spirits, such as strangers never weep.
        Strangers to affections deep.
Haste away to Hagedorn ! and when thou hast embraced him long.
        And that greeting-rapture strong
Is appeased and satisfied, and all the tears of joy are spent
        In the smiles of deep content,
Tell him then, my GIESEKÈ. when three days past the pause allow.
        That I love him e'en as thou.

TO EBERT.

SAD thoughts constrain me from the sparkling bowl,
  EBERT, to melancholy grief.
And ah ! thy words, that erst could cheer my soul,
  Fall idly now, nor bring relief.
I must go forth and weep ! my sorrows crave
  In softening tears to overflow,
For softening tears wise Nature, pitying, gave
  To be companions of our woe.
Were it not so, were tears denied their part,
  Who might endure the painful hour ?
I must go forth and weep ! my swollen heart
  Heaves in me with convulsive power.

EBERT, they all are gone !   All, all our friends
  Lie shadow'd in the crypt and tomb !
We two are here alone : — with us all ends !
  EBERT ! a thought to strike us dumb !

How thy sad eye looks soul-less and distraught !
   So died my troubled sight at first,
So shook I, when that dread o'erwhelming thought
   In sudden thunder on me burst.
As thou the traveller, homeward bound in haste
   To his dear wife, and cultur'd son,
And blooming daughter,—all in thought embrac'd—
   Impetuous thunder, dost outrun,
And seizest with thy death-stroke, and his frame
   A clay-clod in the earth dost roll,
Then piercest, triumphing, the clouds,—so came
   That thought upon my staggering soul,
Till mine eye closed in darkness, and beneath
   My knees sank, failing, to the floor.
In silent night I saw the shades of death,
   Shades of our friends, pass o'er ;
And open'd graves, and, like the vapour's breath,
   The souls of them that die no more.

When GIESEKÈ lives not to smile again,
   When from his RADIKIN remote
Our CRAMER sleeps, where GÄRTNER's, RABNER's, vein
   No more unfolds Socratic thought,

When noble GELLERT his harmonious life
    Has closed, and every chord is dumb ;
And genial ROTHÈ, foe to social strife,
    Seeks out companions o'er the tomb ;
And when to friends from his far exile-place
    Inventive SCHLEGEL writes no more ;
When in my SCHMIDT's, my truest friend's embrace,
    No tears of tenderness I pour ;
When low my FATHER sleeps, and HAGEDORN—
    Oh ! Ebert, what are we who stay ?
We, sons of sorrow, doom'd by Fate forlorn
    To tarry longer than all they !
If one of us should die (my troubled brain
    Still gathers clouds more dark and dun)
If one of us should die, and one remain,
    And I should be that lonely one,
Should she have loved me then, who yet will love,
    And in the grave be laid on sleep,
And I alone upon the earth above
    My solitary pathway keep ;
Wilt thou, O living soul, for friendship made,
    See those drear days with conscious breast ?

Or, maz'd, mistake them for the midnight shade,
    And slumber in oblivious rest?
E'en then thou mightest wake to know thy pain,
    Enduring and undying sprite!
Oh, if thou wakest, call their form again,
    From the cold sepulchre to light.

Graves of the dead,— graves where my friends repose,—
    Why lie ye scatter'd far away?
Nor bid one blooming valley all enclose,
    One grove o'ershade your mingled clay?
Lead me in failing age! with tottering foot
    I will go visit every grave;
A cypress plant, and train the verdant shoot,
    Whose shadow o'er our sons shall wave.
And nightly where the topmost branches sigh
    My dear departed I shall see!
Trembling shall look to heaven, and weep, and die!
    And by the grave, and by the tree
Where I sank down, there let me buried lie!
    Corruption! take my tears and me.

Cease, gloomy thoughts, to thunder in my soul,

　　Awful, and deep, and dread as doom !

My spirit loses, speechless, its control,

　　Nor more can grasp yon thoughts of gloom.

TO FANNY.

WHEN I am dead — when once this mortal frame
    Is moulder'd into dust, and thou mine eye,
So long deploring life's eventful dream,
    In death hast wept thyself for ever dry,

Nor lookest upward while the ages throng
    From thy still adoration ; when my fame,
The fruit of my youth's yearning, and my song,
    And of the love I bore MESSIAH'S name,

Is past and overblown ; or by a few
    In that world rescued from oblivious doom ;
When thou, my Fanny, long hast rested too,
    And gentle smiles no more thine eyes illume ;

When their soul-beaming glance is quench'd and gone,
    And thou, unnoticed by the vulgar crowd,
The work of thy whole life hast nobly done
    In noble deeds, which fame should utter loud,

Worthier remembrance than immortal song!
    Oh, then — albeit in love thou madest thine
A happier — let not the proud word be wrong!
    A happier not a nobler heart than mine;

The day must dawn when I shall live again;
    The day must dawn when thou wilt see the sun;
And envious Fate no more can rend in twain
    The souls whom Nature destined to be one.

Then God shall weigh on the eternal beam
    Virtue and Happiness in equal scales;
And things that struck discordant here shall seem
    Perfect in harmony, where love prevails.

There where thou wakest, in that happy land,
    I will haste to thee. Wander not away
Until some seraph lead me by the hand
    To where thou standest in thy bright array.

Thy brother, welcomed by a dear embrace,
    With me shall seek thee. Joyful tears will stream—
Such tears as glisten on a cherub's face,
    When I stand by thee, call thee by thy name,

And press thee to me. Immortality
    Will all be ours ! O come, ye rapturous train
Of joys unknown to mortal minstrelsy—
    Joys inexpressible, as now my pain!

Ebb then, O life, away ! till comes the hour
    That calls us to the cypress-shade at last ;
Mourning I pine in my deserted bower,
    And see my days with darkness overcast.

PHILOMEL.

ONE joyous spring I burst my bonds and flew.
Upon that joyous spring my mother sweet
    Taught me, and ever did repeat,
      " Sing, Philomel, the spring-tide through.

" When the woods hear, and all the tuneful throng
Flit round thee, listening from their shady sprays,
    Sing then, O Philomel ! the lays
      That but to nightingales belong.

" But if he come, who stands erect and slim,
Like the tall platanus, the lord of earth,
    Sing then a strain of gladder mirth,
      And tuneful as the lyric hymn.

" E'en the immortals hear thee in the grove.
Thy notes evoke their feeling most divine :
    Ah, Philomel, that strain of thine
    Can win immortal hearts to love."

I flew from her and sang ; and all around
The hill and grove with liquid warblings shook,
    And the light babbling of the brook
    Fell on the bank with softer sound.

Yet hill, nor brook, nor oak that proudly nods,
Was that earth-god.   And soon my notes grew faint,
    Because the soft and sweet complaint
    Came not to goddesses or gods.

Then, where like night the deeper shadows lie,
In noble figure fresher than the wealds,
    More blooming than the flow'ry fields,
    Came one of the immortals nigh.

My thrilling bosom glow'd at her advance ;
The west wind held me as I flutter'd low ;
    Oh ! from my throat could music flow
    To tell the rapture of that glance,

Sweeter it were than softest warblings now ;
Sweeter than tenderest notes, when young desire
  Calls me from sprays of fragrant briar
  Up to the forest's topmost bough.

That eye beams on me, an unsetting star !
How art thou named and sung in human song ?
  Art thou the soul, to which belong
  The thoughts that make men, what they are,

Immortal ? Can I find for thee compare ?
Art thou the ethereal blue, when Hesper gleams,
  And soft the golden lustre streams ?
  Or like the brook, that freshly there

Leaps from the fountain ? In the crystal flood
Never the rose-bush saw a fairer sight,
  Never myself I saw more bright,
  When I dropp'd down upon the bud.

What speaks that look ? Dost listen to my strain,
E'en as a nightingale, when soft I sing ?
  What means that dewy glistening
  Which from thine eyes dissolves in rain ?

Love is it that flows fast in gentle showers?
Thy loftiest feelings can my warblings move?
 What soft emotion dost thou prove?
 What influence thy heart o'erpowers?

Oh! happy be thou, blooming twelfth of May!
When that earth-goddess listen'd to my lays;
 But happier thou than all May-days,
 When I shall see her hither stray

Led by some youth, where spring-tide zephyrs call,
Who can those eyes interpret, and so feel
 The sunshine which her smiles reveal,
 And bless the Spirit that made all!

O Fanny! was it not the twelfth of May,
When the shades call'd thee? And to me forlorn
 The evening gather'd on the morn,
 A desolate and dreary day!

THE DEPARTURE.

WHEN sinking into sleep, thou shalt behold
   O'er thee the portal of Eternity,
And see far off the gates of Heaven unfold,
   And where beyond the golden mansions lie ;

And nigh shalt hear the thunder pealing loud,
   That utters forth thy sentence from the Lord,
(For so majestic is the voice of God,
   When He assigns to Virtue her award !)

When nearer thou shalt hear with parting smile
   Thy Salem's[1] voice, that did thy steps attend,
And 'mid the seraph's softest tones, the while,
   Discern'st the voice of thy departed friend ;

[1] The name of a guardian angel.

Long ere that day I shall have found my rest,
    And spoken, the last evening, as I leant,
With many a tear, upon thy brother's breast,
    My hand in his hand sunk, with sweet content,—

My Schmidt, I die! and round me soon shall know
    The lofty souls celestial fame embalms;[2]
Adam with him who sang of Adam's woe,
    And Eve beside him, with her crown of palms

Inwreath'd for Milton's brow: with them the meek,
    The pious Singer; Radikin, too, there;
And him whose death to me did strangely speak,
    " Affliction comes, nor life is always fair,"—

My brother,[3] who bloom'd sweetly but not long!
    Soon I shall gain my spirits' far desire,
And mingle with the hallelujah song,
    And hear the harpings of the seraph quire.

[2] Pope and Addison are named in the original.

[3] " A little before his death, when he was not yet six years old, he went out one day in the midst of a heavy thunder-storm, and stood with his head uncovered. When his father called to him, he replied, ' I am worshipping the Great God.' "

Well is me ! for my bosom burns, and strong
  Through all my frame the kindling rapture glows.
Well is me ! for the soul for ever young
  With thoughts that talk with angels overflows.

Half lost to life, my weary limbs revive.
  So shall I rise, and breathe a freer breath.
Deep awe with thrilling ravishment shall strive,
  When I awake with thee from silent death.

My heart beats softly : there, my friend, repose !
  I lived, and that I lived feel no regret.
I lived to thee, to friends my bosom chose,
  But yet to Him, whose judgment-seat is set.

I hear far off the clanking of the scale,
  And Justice speaking with the voice of God ;
Oh ! might the holier thoughts and deeds prevail !
  Oh ! might the better be the heavier load !

I sang to men, as man, the Eternal King,
  GOD, THE REDEEMER !   Underneath the throne
Lies my august reward, which angels bring,
  A golden bowl with Christian tears o'erflown.

Oh, glorious hours ! oh, sad, but glorious time !
  To me how sacred, which with thee I pass'd.
The first flow'd freely by in youthful prime,
  The first went smiling, but I wept the last.

More than mine eye can tell thee, loved my heart ;
  More my heart loved thee than its sighs avow.
Leave off thy weeping, else I shall depart ;
  Up ! be a man ! go, and love ROTHE now !

I might not live on earth the life of heaven.
  Therefore she loved me not, I loved so well.
Go, thou who knowest how my heart was riven,
  Go, when I die, and to thy sister tell,—

Not those sad hours of unforgotten tears ;
  Nor, like the night-fall of a gloomy day,
The brief conclusion of my troubled years,
  O'erdrawn with clouds that would not pass away ;

Nor how I wept in sadness on thy breast,
  Dumb with my grief ! Blest be thou, friend most dear,
Because thou sharedst all my heart's unrest,
  And in my sorrow mingledst tear for tear !

Haply some maiden, listener to my rhyme,
   And noble-hearted, on some future day
Will round her draw the noblest of her time,
   And there in melancholy sadness say,

" Would he were living still, whose wounded heart
   So felt love's power !" And she will hold thee dear,
Because in my deep anguish thou hadst part,
   And mingledst in my sorrow tear for tear.

Go to thy sister, Schmidt, when I am dead ;
   Speak not of grief, go smiling as I died.
Tell her that, while the death-shade o'er me spread,
   I thus spoke to her, and my tears were dried.—

Oh ! tell her my heart's language, if my gaze,
   Darkening in death, its meaning may convey—
" How I have loved thee ! how to thee my days
   All consecrate have pass'd unmark'd away !"

O sister of the best of brothers, take
   The parting blessing which thy friend can give ;
No man that lived on thee such blessing spake,
   To speak such blessing none shall ever live.

With the high meed that waits the pure in heart,
 With all the bliss celestial spirits know,
With that calm peace true virtue can impart,
 Be thy heart full, and, godlike, overflow !

Thou must weep tears of human sympathy,
 Sad tears and many, when the sufferer's woes
Before thee lie reveal'd : and visibly
 The form to thy companions shalt disclose

Of saintly Virtue,—fairest of God's works,
 Unrecognised below ; and joys divine
In whose festivity no sadness lurks,
 Shall, jubilant, thy youthful head entwine :—

For thee prepared, when from thy Maker's hand
 Thou camest with thy smile so fair to see,
And He, whose gift thou couldst not understand,
 Gave to thee joys serene, and tears to me.

Fair soul ! how deep, how earnest was my love !
 But from the dust devoutly, while I grieve,
Him I adore, who sits all fair above,
 Fairer than fairest angel can conceive.

When I fall prostrate in His presence there,
   And, deep-adoring, bow before His throne,
Breathing, with outstretch'd arms, for thee a prayer,
   In stammering words to earthly sense unknown,

Then shall some yearnings of the infinite,
   Some soft and thrilling sense of angels' good,
Some sweet emotions of their pure delight,
   Stream on thy soul in an o'erwhelming flood.

And thou wilt upward raise thy wondering sight,
   And smile to the bright heavens that o'er thee rise.
Oh then, come quickly in thy raiment white,
   Wafted on waves of light through the clear skies!"

I spake : mine eye upon her likeness fell,
   And so I died.   He saw me as I lay,
And blamed her not—because he loved her well—
   That his true friend was snatch'd so soon away.

When thus my days have reach'd their destined end,
   And thou, my Fanny, too, art near to die,
How wilt thou meet the memory of thy friend?
   That solemn hour,—what will thy heart reply ?

How wilt thou think of him who nobly felt
    And wholly loved thee?   How, of midnight hours,
When Sorrow and Despair together dwelt?
    How of the blasting of his spirit's powers?

How of that sadness, when his youthful love,
    By thee scarce noticed, pleaded to thine eyne,
And, not too proud, in silence sought to prove
    That Nature's self had form'd his soul for thine?

What thoughts will come, when o'er thy shoulder thou
    Throw'st back on life a fleet but earnest glance?
A noble heart was thine, I dare avow,
    Worthy a better fate than such mischance!

Die gently! with hands folded on thy breast!
    Thou, whom I loved with love beyond compare!
Sleep sweetly! sink into eternal rest,
    E'en as God made thee, innocent and fair!

HOURS OF DEDICATION.

WELCOME, sweet Hours, that with the star of eve
Glimmer serene, with holy fancies fraught,
Pass not away ! your wonted blessing leave,
    And bring me some ennobling thought.

There spake a Spirit in the gate of heaven :
" Haste, holy Hours, that from these portals high
To men who dwell on earth are rarely given,
    Haste to that youth of pensive eye,

Who God the Saviour sings to Adam's race ;
O'ershadow him, while silent Night invades,
With golden wings, that lonely he may trace
    Bright forms amid the heavenly shades.

What ye produce, still Hours, shall hoary Time
(So Salem tells) to distant ages give.
While men adore with rapture more sublime
    MESSIAS, and more holy live."

He spake : and through my bones responsively
Thrill'd the deep echo of that Spirit's voice.
I stood, as when in thunder God goes by,
　　And bids me marvel and rejoice !

Be here no prating sermoniser known !
Hither no stiff and formal Christian come
Who feels not his own prophets !　Every tone
　　That speaks not things divine, be dumb !

Veil the still entrance with your sacred night,
Sweet Hours, nor let a human step draw near !
Warn e'en away those friendly footfalls light,
　　That sound so welcome and so dear.

Save only when to me my Schmidt would come
From sweet society of Zion's muse :
So he converse but of the Judgment doom,[1]
　　Or his high sister's thoughts infuse.

[1] He contemplated at this time a poem on the **Last** Judgment.

In her e'en censure wears a winning grace.
And what her heart and finer sense have never
Felt in our lays, be blotted from its place!

 What she hath felt there stand for ever!

TO GOD.[1]

A SECRET awe doth through my bosom steal
    Of the All-present God.   Gently my heart
Heaves up within me, and I feel—I feel
    Thou too art here—here where I weep Thou art!

And from Thy countenance, Eternal Being,
    Beams the dread glance that looks my spirit thro',
Holy be thou before the Great All-seeing,
    My soul, whose breath from His breath being drew.

---

[1] This, and some other personal odes, were not originally
intended for publication; but being privately circulated among
Klopstock's friends, it soon became necessary to publish them
in a correct form to prevent the multiplication of spurious
copies.

Am I deceived ? or shall my lips declare
  What thought in whispers doth to thought rehearse ?
Is the persuasion real, that I dare
  Free with the Maker of my soul converse ?

O thoughts which in the Eternal Mind abide,
  If ye be angry with the thoughts of men,
Ah, whither from your presence shall they hide,
  And whither flee, where ye come not again ?

Down to the pit ? behold, ye too are there !
  Or if they hasten into boundless space,
Beyond the circles of the ambient air,
  Ye are all-seeing eyes in every place.

Or if they take the wings of seraphim,
  And upward soar to the celestial choirs,
'Mid echoes of the Hallelujah Hymn,
  And the loud tones of the eternal lyres,

Then would ye hear them, Auditors Divine !
  Then flee no longer : rest within the sphere
Of human sympathies ! a narrow line
  High Heaven hath set about your rovings here.

E

Oh ! the glad confidence, the solace dear,

   That my soul dares with Thee, my God, to speak !

That my lips dare to pour into Thine ear

   The thoughts of man in stammering voices weak.

Yes, I will speak to Thee ! but Thou know'st well

   The secret grief that doth my bones consume ;

Long hast Thou known the thoughts that in me dwell,

   And make my bosom their perpetual tomb,

Not first to-day Thou saw'st my moments fly,

   To me long painful years of broken trust :

E'en what Thou wast Thou art eternally,

   Thou art Jehovah ! I am dust of dust.

Dust, yet immortal ! for the living fire

   Thou gavest, Thou hast given me for ever.

Thy breath that breathed Thy likeness did inspire

   Yearnings of boundless bliss and high endeavour !

A countless throng ! But brighter than the rest

   One stood alone, and, other powers above,

Reign'd as a queen — the last trait, and the best,

   That perfected Thy likeness,— holy love !

Thou feel'st it as may feel the Ever-blest.

 They feel it, whom celestial raptures move,

The angelic hosts — the last trait, and the best,

 That perfected Thy likeness — holy love !

Deeply Thou gravedst it in Adam's heart,

 When, to his full idea of perfect grace,

Fashion'd to be of all his being part,

 Thou ledd'st to him the mother of our race.

And deeply it was graven in my heart.

 But, to my full idea of perfect grace,

Fashion'd to be of all my being part,

 Her whom I loved Thou hidest from my face.

Her unto whom I pour'd out my whole soul,

 In all the tears that sorrow taught to flow,

To whom the tide of all my thoughts did roll —

 Whom I so loved,— Thou takest from me now.

Tak'st by Thy destiny, that still transforms

 Before my sight, and in the darkness wanes ;

Tak'st far away from my extended arms,

 Not from my heart, which yet the more complains.

Thou knowest the far-purpose of Thy will
   In its first thought, ere yet it stood complete
By Thy creative power, when Thou didst seal
   Souls with one image — for each other meet.

Thou knowest it, Creator ; yet Thy Fate
   Severs the souls created to be one.
So high and so inscrutable Thy state !
   So dark Thy will ! — and yet that will be done !

Life in the presence of Eternity
   Is like the breath that from the dying flees,
Wherewith the soul flows forth, no more to die,
   Mingling for ever with the eternal seas.

When once the sire of Fate resolves in light
   Its labyrinths, and Fate prevails no more,
Oh ! then what ravishment shall reunite
   Disparted souls, when human change is o'er !

That thought is worthy the immortal soul !
   Worthy to mitigate enduring woe !
My spirit rises, with its greatness full ;
   But ah ! too much I feel this life below.

What was a breath seems fearfully to swim
  In dread immensity before my sight!
I see, I see my sorrows, drear and dim,
  Expand into illimitable night!

E'en as a breath, O God, my life receive!
  Nay! — rather give me her who should be mine!
Oh! give her! It is light for Thee to give!
  Give to the heart, whose days in sadness pine.

Give to the trembling that goes forth to meet her, —
  To the still voice that pleads in the heart's cell,
And, speechless of its feelings, can but greet her
  With tears, which somewhat of its language tell.

Give to these arms, which oft to heaven above
  I raised in childhood, innocently blest,
And pray'd with brow of reverential love,
  Safe to be taken to eternal rest!

One nod of Thine bestows: then from the worm,
  Whose hours are ages, soon the gift recalls —
Recalls from the poor worm of human form,
  Whose greatness buds and blooms, o'erblooms and falls.

By her beloved, I will name Virtue fair
    And happy.   I will gaze upon her mien
With fix'd, unwandering eyes ; and seek out there,
    Where her look points, the blissful and serene.

But, O diviner Virtue, that dost dwell
    Farther and higher in thy bright abode,
Thee will I honour, too, with purer zeal,
    Unknown and unobserved by all but God.

By her beloved, more fervidly my tongue
    Shall sing and laud Thy name.   And I will pour
My heart into that hallelujah song
    And Thee, Eternal Father, will adore.

Then when with me she lifts her prayer to heaven,
    Adoring Thy great Name through many a tear,
Already I shall feel to me 'tis given,
    With her to lead the life of angels here.

The harp of Zion, resting on her arm,
    I will strike, raptured, with sublimer sweep :
The good shall hear, who own affection's charm,—
    Christians who love like us, like us can weep.

HENRY THE FOWLER.

THE foe is there! the fight begins!
  Up! to the victory speed!
The heart — the hand — in all the land
  The best, is here to lead!

He feels not faint to day.   With pride
  They bear him to the van.
Hail, Henry, hail! in iron mail
  A hero and a man!

His forehead flush'd with glory's glow,
  Rules where the banners wave.
The dews of blood around him stud
  The helmets of the brave.

Flash, sword, with dread and dazzling gleams,
　　Round Cæsar's hand on high !
That missile fleet and arrowy sleet
　　May pass him, scathless, by.

Welcome is death for Fatherland.
　　When bleeding droops our head,
We sink to rest by patriots bless'd
　　On honour's gory bed.

When lies an open field before,
　　And all the dead lie round,
Then we who stand for Fatherland
　　With glory's wreath are crown'd.

Then we stalk proudly o'er the field
　　With dead and dying strown ;
And, 'mid the rout, the victory shout
　　Rings through the marrow and bone.

They praise us with impetuous joy—
　　The bridegroom and the bride.
He sees on high the banners fly,
　　And clasps her to his side.

And speaks to her: Ah! there they come,
   The crested heroes see!
They staked their life in battle-strife,
   My bride, for thee and me!

They praise us through their glittering tears—
   The mother and her child:
Close to her breast the boy she press'd,
   And on the Cæsar smiled.

Renown is ours that ever lives,
   When we have spent our breath—
A faithful band—for Fatherland
   In honourable death.

THE BRIDE.

Not for the songs of pleasant pastime born,
Nor meet to meditate the Cnidian strain,
The wish o'ercame me once, and I was fain
　　To sing like Schmidt and Hagedorn.

Already lost, my wand'ring hand, O fair,
Felt for Anacreon's touch ; and on the lyre
The silver tones ran down the trembling wire,
　　That told of flowing flaxen hair,—

Of stolen kiss, that wins but half its worth ;
Of sweeter rapture of the boon allow'd ;
Of youths and maidens circling through the crowd
　　Their whisperings of frolic mirth,

When the fleet music flies along the room
Impetuous,—lending pinions to the dance,
And round the maiden throws a wilder glance,

    In breathless ecstasy o'ercome ;—

Of softer heavings of the bosom coy,
That fain would see, unwilling to be seen ;
And of what else to festive bards has been

    The life of songs that move to joy.

But, with an earnest look sedate, on mine
The Muse—my Muse, URANIA—turn'd her eyes,
Like Singer, deep of thought and heavenly wise :

    Or, Fanny, like thy glance divine.

Sing, she spake to me, that which Nature taught !
To thee such songs did Nature ne'er inspire.
With Friendship's glow, with Virtue's holy fire,

    The burden of *thy* song be fraught !

She spake, and mounted the Olympic height.
But shall her form, so grave and earnest, dare,
'Mid sounds of mirth and maidens blooming fair,

    Cross the gay scene with footfall light ?

Yes! For thou hear'st me in thy bridal guise;
Thy cultured heart can mingle grave with gay,
Quaffing a deeper joy from smiles that play
 Benignantly in Virtue's eyes.

When blooms the vernal lip, the cheek, no more;
When our beclouded gaze is lost in night;
When, wise at last, on Folly's vain delight
 The look of cold contempt we pour;

And, where the Spring once call'd us to its bloom,
Grandsons and daughters there, our graves above,
No more rememb'ring us, each other love,—
 Then Virtue triumphs o'er the tomb.

That Virtue crowns thee with thy modest grace,
And blesses him whom thy affections choose,
While tears of joy thy mother's eyes infuse,
 Looking in love upon thy face!

TO BODMER.

Who rules the Fates, disperses oft in air
   Pure vows and golden visions fair,
And, where we fain an even path would tread,
   Bids a dark lab'rinth round us spread,
God sees far oft the unnumber'd ages rise
   Invisible to mortal eyes.
Ah! they meet not—until they meet above—
   Souls that were form'd for mutual love!
Some are dissever'd by remoter climes,
   And some by wide-disparted times.
Mine eye ne'er saw Socratic Addison,
   His voice was to my ear unknown;
Nor Singer smiled on me—enchantress sweet-
   Round whom the dead and living meet.

Nor thee shall I behold, whose yearning breast,
    Long after I am laid on rest,
Made after mine own heart, and likest mine,
    Shall for our spirits' union pine.
I shall not aught of all thy being ken,
    Unless I be thy GENIUS then.
So God ordains, who sees the years afar
    That shall be, as the years that are.
Oft, too, He fills our cup of blessing higher
    Than our full heart had dared desire.
We see our joys as waking from a dream,
    And scarce believe they more than seem.
So joy'd I when I found me, face to face,
    Welcomed by Bodmer's warm embrace.

THE LAKE OF ZURICH.

O MOTHER NATURE, beautiful and bright
Is all thy work o'er mountain, vale, and sea!
  Brighter the eye that drinks delight
  From lofty communings with thee!

Come from the vine-shores of the glimmering lake,
Sweet joys! or, if the fading earth ye leave,
  Come from the rosy tints, that break
  O'er the far West, on wings of eve.

Come, and my lay with youthful rapture fill,
Glad as the voice of blithesome shepherd-boy,
  Whose carols wake the echoes shrill,
  Yet gentle, as my Fanny's joy.

Uto we left behind us, at whose feet
Zurich, recumbent, rears her freeborn sons;
   And many a slope with vines replete
   Back from our gaze receding runs.

Already rose the silver Alpine cones
Unclouded.   Our young hearts more warmly beat,
   And spoke in more impassion'd tones
   To Doris, our companion sweet;

Who sang — herself well worthy of the strain —
Our Hirzel's " Daphne," whom Kleist loves as Gleim :
   And we pour'd forth our glad refrain
   And felt, like Hagedorn, sublime.

But soon the Au received us in the arms
Of the cool-shading wood that crown'd the isle.
   There, there thou shower'dst down thy charms,
   Bright Joy, and badest all things smile !

O Joy divine, thee, thee, we deeply felt
Thou camest, sister of Humanity !
   Together in our hearts ye dwelt
   In glad and blameless harmony.

Sweet is thine inspiration, when the ground
Blooms to thee, joyous Spring ! and, incense-laden,
 Thy balmy breath is pour'd around
 Into the heart of youth and maiden.

The feeling that o'ermasters thou dost move,
And glowing bosoms deeper breath respire.
 The spell that bound the lips of love
 Thou brakest with thy touch of fire.

The wine winks brightly to the genial soul :
But dearer is the joy, when sparkles round
 Pure thought from the Socratic bowl
 With wreaths of dewy roses crown'd :

When the heart swells, and high resolve is born
Of spirits who the sottish herd despise ;
 Learning in converse high to scorn
 The thought unworthy of the wise.

Alluringly the silver tone of Fame
Rings in the throbbing heart. To live for ever
 Is a great thought,—a noble aim,
 Worthy the toil of high endeavour !

F

To linger by the power of living song
With children's children, sons and daughters dear ;
　　Oft to be named with raptured tongue,
　　Oft in our graves their call to hear ;

And then to form their tender hearts to love,
To mould their tender hearts to Virtue's sway,—
　　This is a meed our souls to move,
　　And worthy of our proud assay !

But deeper is the charm—more true and sweet,
To know me, in my friend's embrace, a friend ;
　　And taste a life not all unmeet
　　To fill the days that shall not end.

Fann'd by soft airs beneath the shady wood,
With tender feeling, and dejected eye
　　That pored upon the silver flood,
　　I breathed a wish with silent sigh.

Would ye were here who love me far away,
Dispersed in vales of dear paternal ground,—
　　Whom in life's happy dawn of day
　　My yearning spirit sought and found !

Oh! we would build our huts of friendship here,
And live and linger till the ages fail!
   This wood should be our Tempè dear,
    And our Elysium yonder vale.

FREDERIC THE FIFTH

(OF DENMARK).

WHAT king the God of Kings, when he was born,
Look'd on, and seal'd with consecrating hand,
Him shall the title " Friend of Man " adorn,
    And " Father of his Fatherland."

Too dearly bought with blood of blooming sons,
With midnight tears of mother and of wife,
Immortal fame in vain with silver tones
    Allures him to the field of strife.

Before the conqueror's bust he never shed
The tears of envy.   To his noble heart,
Soon as with human sympathies it bled,
    Too narrow was the conqueror's part.

But tears for nobler fame that lives aloft,—
Tears to be loved, beyond the flatterer's boon,
By a contented people, waked him oft
    At night, in the still hour of noon ;

When slept the suckling on the mother's breast
To happy manhood rising on her dreams.
And when the " Father of his people " blest
    The old man's slumber with bright gleams.

He muses long, how noble is the right
To govern like the Godhead, and create
Blessings for thousands : He has reach'd a height
    Where God he dares to imitate.

As awfully that great and dreadful day
Weighs in the balance princes when they die,
So would he first in his own bosom weigh
    The deeds that write his destiny.

He reigns a Christian, and rewards the good,
Then smiles on those that meditate the Muse,
Whose gentle influence refines the rude
    And with sublimer thoughts imbues.

To mute desert that lingers in the shade
He beckons, and unfolds the way to fame ;
For he has trod without the Muse's aid
    The pathway to a deathless name.

O Muse divine, that down from Sion's hill
God the Messiah singest to the crowd,
Haste to the heights, where harps their raptures fill
    To kings who imitate their God.

The lyric strain with his renown begin,
Whose name, resounding, trembles on the strings
Oft as thou tell'st the noble deeds that win
    High blessing on the throne of kings.

'Tis Denmark's Fred'ric ! who with flowers has strown
The lofty path, O Muse, which thou must tread.
A king, a Christian, bids thee lead him on
    To Golgotha where Jesus bled.

CLARISSA DEAD.

Sweet flower, that dost, transplanted, bloom,
Unmeet to grow in earthly gloom,
Meet to fade soon — beyond the tomb
    Reserved for Eden bowers ;

Airs such as these o'er land and sea —
The gentlest — are too rude for thee.
One cruel storm (oh, haste and flee,
    Ere it rush down in showers)

Will blast thee in thy brightest gleam :
Yet, even blasted, thou wilt seem
So beautiful, our tears will stream,
    Wondering to see the dead.

Lovely and fair for evermore
She lay, when all her bloom was o'er.
And still her cheek so sunken bore
 Tints of its native red.

Gladly her parting soul had flown
To join the spirits like her own ;
Bright kindred spirits, dearly known,
 Who gave her welcome there,

Where, straightway, song melodious fills
The balmy air among the hills.
Rest and the crown reward thine ills,
 O soul that wert so fair !

They who were worthy thus have reapt.
Come, Cisly, let the hour be kept,
When so sublime she look'd, and slept,
 In sacred festival !

Bring cypress, that for sorrow's bower
I may twine wreaths ! that solemn hour
Thine eyes a sisterly sweet shower
 Shall on those wreaths let fall.

FREDERIC THE FIFTH

TO BERNSTORFF AND MOLTKE.

Now where the ice-clad mountains veil'd in night,
   And where the lonely woodlands waste
Silent repose, I thither I speed my flight,
   And wingèd thoughts before me haste
To you, my friends, worthy the best of kings.
   His name my lyre did lightly thrill,
But now to you from a full heart she brings
   The feelings that my bosom fill.
In no ambiguous tone I dare proclaim,
   That to the conqueror at Sorr
Too mean is Julian, and a Christian name
   Our Frederic worthy bore.

Dark were the thought that such he would not be !
　　When his friend heard the angel's call,
And surely knew, from darkling mazes free,
　　That Jesus reigns and judges all,
True to himself he smiled ; yet smiling wept
　　O'er the dear friend whose soul was flown,
And, when the lines were changed, aside he stept,
　　And fain would be unseen, alone.

Leave, serious Muse, the thoughts of whelming woe,
　　And joyous bid the lyre tell forth
In tones as when the silver fountains flow
　　The pride of the Teutonic North.
They speak of honour who but Frederic name !
　　Nations shall call him The Beloved,
And sages, scrupulous of praise and blame,
　　Shall find no life like his approved
That dreadful day, which Zion's Muse assay'd
　　E'en here with stammering voice to sing,
When in Fame's temple all the laurels fade,
　　And Honour no defence can bring,—
That dreadful day shall stand before the Lord,
E'en as his life was, his reward.

FRIEDENSBURG.

THE very angel leaves the Elysian groves,
Leaves his bright coronet before the throne,
 And here in youthful semblance roves
 As man among his fellows known.

Cease then, O Muse ! to sing of judgment-doom,
Of kings that fell with their disjected crown ;
 Come where these vales of verdant bloom
 Invite thee to their Tempè down.

Come ! for their smile awaits thee !   Where on high
The cedars waver to thy song of might ;
 Not there alone expanded lie
 The fields of ravishing delight !

Here, too, did Nature tarry, when her hand
Pour'd living beauty over dale and hill ;
    And to adorn this pleasant land
    Long time she linger'd and stood still.

The lake, how tranquil !   From its level brim
The shore swells gently, wooded o'er with green,
    And buries in its verdure dim
    The lustre of the summer e'en.

See where the woods, umbrageous, wave on high !
Is't to the breath of the awakening breeze ?
    Nay ; but o'er Frederic, passing by,
    Wave the high branches of the trees !

Angel, why smiles thy look ?   Why gleams around
This joy and ravishment from eyes so calm ?
    Say, doth his name already sound
    Celebrious, where expands the palm ?

"Think'st thou that, wakeful, our deep-searching eyes
See not the things which on the earth ye do ?
    Nor can the noble recognise,
    So sever'd from the crowd and few ?

" We who, before it buds, the thought descry ;
By whom far off the coming deed is seen,
    E'en yet it dawn upon the eye,
    While yet it wears another mien ?

" Is aught to us more noble than a king
Who, young and ardent, yet is wisely just ?
    Around whose temples honours cling,
    Which he that wears makes more august ?

" When comes the hour, whose thunder voice is sent
To smite from kingly heads the jewell'd toy,
    Unmoved he hears it with content,
    And slumbers into dreamless joy.

" Around him gather'd stand his holy deeds :
Each wears a glorious halo, light bestrown ;
    And each—a gentle handmaid—leads
    His spirit to the judgment-throne."

THE TRANSFORMED.

Long time by grief o'erwhelm'd the love I learn'd,
Which earth forsook, yet, whilome, from above
    To Virtue's secret home return'd,
    Like her who earliest woke to love,

And, full of innocence and youthful hope,
Came to the shore with breath of balmy air ;
    And with the roses from the slope
    Saw in the flood her reflex fair.

To me she came. O Grief ! when she was near,
Why with thy stroke so stunning didst thou smite ?
    Filling my heart with trembling fear,
    And broodings gloomy as the night.

Years hast thou smitten me.   At last the hours
Of darkness into morn unhoped for break :
  And with bright smile the dormant powers
  Of joy, that slumber'd long, awake.

Are ye the same ? or is my heart betray'd ?
Oh, no ! the peace, the feeling, soft as this
  Which does my being all pervade,
  I felt in those first days of bliss !

Oh, how I marvel I again should be
The thing I was !   How do the turns of fate
  Hold me amazed !   How thankfully
  My heart within me leaps elate !

Nothing ignoble, no disdain of heart,
No deaden'd feeling gives me this repose.
  Is it, O Virtue ! that thou art
  The sweet rewarder of my woes ?

Is it thou only ? or (oh, that I dare
Trust my own thought !) descends not from thine height
  A maiden, led by thee, and fair
  As Innocence, to greet my sight ?

Gentle in dreams, and gentler when I wake!
To her, before the vision flits away,
  With broken, stammering voice I speak,—
  " Why fleest thou?   I love thee—stay !"

My heart thou knowest, how it loved and strove.
Know'st thou its like?   Perchance 'tis thine alone.
  So love me, Cisly, for the love
  I whilome learnt for thee unknown.

Yes, to find thee, I learnt the mighty power
That elevated and enlarged my heart ;
  Which now, in dreams, to Eden's bower
  Conducts me, Cisly, where thou art.

TO THE REDEEMER.

THE seraph stammers ; and the fields on high
　　Tremble through all their circuit to prolong
Thy praise supreme, O Son !　And who am I,
　　That I should dare to mingle with the song ?

Dust of the dust !　Yet in this ruin dwells
　　A spirit that from lofty lineage came,
And thinks the thoughts whose tide of rapture swells
　　Through all the pulses of my thrilling frame.

More than a ruin thou shalt one day be,
　　O earth-built home that dost the soul o'ershade ;
And other raptures, holier ecstasy,
　　Shall wake thee where in slumber thou art laid.

G

Thou stage of life and field of our decay,

 Where Adam's son shall be as erst his sire,

When from creating arms he burst away

 Exulting, and did living breath respire ;

Thou field, that art replete with holy dead

 From day-dawn to the far-descending sun,

When shall I see thee ? when the teardrops shed,

 Which with the thousand thousand tears shall run ?

Ye hours—or ages—of oblivious sleep,

 Pass quickly o'er ! pass o'er, that I may rise !

Ah ! ye are distant ! and my path I keep

 This side the grave, and far beneath the skies.

Handmaid of peace, bright hour of death, O come !

 Where art thou, garden of all-hallow'd ground,

Where this life ripens to immortal bloom,

 Nor dearer soil for heavenly seed is found ?

Oh ! let me go, that I may see the spot,

 That I may gaze on it with raptur'd eye,

And strew with harvest flowers the cherish'd plot,

 And lay me down amid the flowers and die !—

A wish of bright expectancy, to those
　To whom that hour with blessedness shall flow
Full to their hearts' desire! Who so repose
　In blissful death, no equal have below.

Then would I mingle, bolder and more blest,
　The voice of man with the angelic choir,
And holier sing whom my soul loves,— the best
　Of woman-born, Son of the Eternal Sire!

Yet let me live, till I have reach'd the goal,
　And sung to men my consecrated lay;
Then die! that, dying, my triumphant soul
　Far o'er the grave may wing its lofty way!

O Thou, my Master, who didst high unfold
　The Godhead, let me not the pathway miss
By which Thou wentest; where Thy prophets old,
　The heralds of Thy glory, sang of bliss!

There all is heavenly! From the depth of night,
　Where Thou didst tread, I follow on Thy trace,
And glimmering glory from Thy radiant height
　Streams downward, visibly, before my face.

My spirit thirsts for immortality !
   Not that which fades so soon on this drear land,
But for the palms that spring beyond the sky,
   Which the Redeemèd bear in their right hand.

Shew me the life-course, at whose distant bourne
   The palm-branch waves ! The thoughts that highest soar
Exalt in me more highly !   Bid them learn
   The truths that shall be truths for evermore !

That I their deathless echoes may proclaim
   To mortal men ! and, ere my spirit faints,
With hallow'd hand take from God's altar flame,
   And pour the flame into the heart of saints.

QUEEN LUISA.

(CONSORT OF FREDERIC THE FIFTH.)

WHEN she, whose name is heard in heaven alone,
   Closed in still death her gentle eyes,
And from her throne up to a higher throne
    Did in white raiment rise,

We wept. E'en he, whose tears did rarely come,
   Turn'd pale, and shook, and wept aloud ;
Who deeper felt stood motionless and dumb,
    Then wept, in silence bowed.

So stands the marble o'er the grave for aye ;
   So Frederic gazed upon her track ;
Her angel, as he bore his charge away,
    Upon his tears look'd back.

Oh ! sorrow strong as death ! We should not weep,
  Because she died so great and good !
Yet the tears fall.   How does a love so deep
    In blessing o'er her brood !

The King look'd on her, as in death she lay :
  His son slept death-still at her side.
He, too, O God ! he snatch'd so soon away,
    In whom a Frederic died !

Weeping we worship.   Since her life no more
  May teach us, learn we from her death !
Learn from that wonderful and heavenly hour,
    When God recall'd her breath.

That hour of death shall children's children keep,
  A fast at midnight through long years ;—
With hallow'd musings and emotions deep,
    A festival of tears !

Nor that alone : she died through many days,
  And every day the death forecast,
So full of high instruction and of praise,
    With which she died at last.

The solemn hour drew near, in misty pall,
With which it shrouds the graves at e'en :
The Queen alone could hear the light footfall
Of those who came unseen.

Alone, that night, she heard the rush of wings,
Heard with a smile the death-tone sound :
Glad and triumphant be my lay that sings
That smile of peace profound !

Now thrones are nothing, nothing more is great
Of all that glitters 'neath the sun.
Twin teardrops fall ; one for her consort's fate,
And for her children one,

And for her mother, loving and belov'd ;
And then God only fills her breast.
The earth sinks from her, as light dust remov'd,
And now—she sleeps in rest !

She sleeps in death.   Bright beams the seraph's eye,
Who bears her to the Lord of all.
Her cheek grows pale and sinks ; the teardrops dry,
The last that did not fall.

Bright is the patriot's honourable wound ;
  Brighter the death the Christian dies ;
Brighter the pure last rest, the sleep profound,
    That seals his weary eyes.

Few can forecast for him what honours wait
  Who rests victorious from the strife,
Who, to his God for ever consecrate,
    Shall rise to nobler life.

Wake then a song of high immortal aim,
  Nor longer sing of dust, my lyre !
Her dust is holy : but the spirit's flame
    Burns with a holier fire.

She stood before her God.   Her seraph-guide
  Stood there, the guardian of her land :
And golden rays stream'd round her from the side,
    Where Caroline did stand.

The mighty daughter down from her new throne
  Saw where with kings they made her grave ;
Look'd on the seraph, and with gentle tone
    These words she, blissful, gave :

My guide, who leddest me this glorious way
    To joys remote from earthly sorrow,
If thou return to where we die to-day
      And deathless are to-morrow;

If thou return to where thou didst befriend
    My consort's and my country's right,
I will go with thee — will with thee attend,
      And be his guardian sprite.

When thou invisible the spot shalt seek,
    Where lonely he bewails my death,
I too will soothe his grief, and gently speak
      These thoughts with whispering breath :

When thou, my king, dost feel a life serene
    Stream on thy soul with holy calm,
Know that 'twas I, who on thy soul, unseen,
      Poured down that heavenly balm.

Oh, that this hand, these locks resplendent, were
    But visible to thee below !
Then should this hand, these locks of golden hair,
      Dry up thy tears that flow.

Weep not! For them that pity human dole
   There lives on high a glorious boon,
A great reward, and crowns about the goal,
     Which I have reach'd so soon.

Thou followest those, who for the palm-branch ran ;
   But longer does thy course incline.
Humanity, the noblest praise of man,
     That bliss and praise are thine.

I hover near each day thou mak'st renown'd,
   By deeds humane, thy whole life through.
This is the meed the early dead have found,
     To see the deeds ye do.

One day so spent is more than many lives
   That down to waste oblivion run.
Who nobly rules, though young he die, survives
     The work of ages done.

I write each deed—and brightly shone her look,
   And heavenly-smiling high she stood—
I write each deed in the great Angel's Book,
     And name it before God !

HERMANN AND THUSNELDA.[1]

HA! there he comes, bedeck'd with gore,
With dust and sweat from Roman fight!
Never look'd Hermann's eyes so bright,
    So beautiful, before!

Come! my heart leaps within my breast!
Reach me the dripping sword, the shield:
Come, breathless, from the dreadful field,
    Come to these arms and rest!

[1] HERMANN, the ARMINIUS of Tacitus, the son of SIGMAR,
the chief of the Cherusci, delivered his country by the rout and
slaughter of the Roman army under Varus, A.D. 9. He carried
off THUSNELDA, the daughter of SEGISTUS, chief of the Catti, and
married her against her father's will.

Rest here, that I may wipe thy brow,
Thy glowing cheek, from blood and sweat !
O Hermann, Hermann, never yet
    Thusnelda loved as now.

Not e'en when first, where oak-shades frown,
Thy brawny arm embraced me wild.
Fleeing, I stay'd with thee, and smil'd
    To see thy far renown.

Tell it in all the woods — to-day
Augustus sips the nectar sad :
For Hermann, Hermann's brow is clad
    With wreaths that bloom for aye.

" Why dost thou twine in locks my hair ?
Sleeps not our sire supine and dead ?
Oh, had the host Augustus led,
    He had lain bloodier there ! "

Nay, let me part the hairs that clot,
That round thy wreath the locks may fall !
SIGMAR reclines in ODIN's hall.
    Follow, but weep him not.

EXPOSTULATION.

Scorn him, my song, who feels no native fire,
  Who, all unmeet to strive for Albion's crown,
Unmeet for nobler aims, would fain aspire
  By distant imitation to renown !

Shall Hermann's son, while Leibnitz' laurels bloom,
  (The sage's life lives with us to this day !)
Shall he in fetters follow those, to whom
  He might with bolder daring shew the way ?

Nor feel his cheek deep-dyed with burning shame ?
  When he beholds the Greek's Mæonian flight,
Shall he not once with ardent voice exclaim,—
  Was he alone born with a poet's right ?

Shall he not weep for anger and despite?
  Weep for ambition, if his voice be dumb?
At midnight rave? and the foul wrong requite
  In works that shall avenge the years to come?

True, the fierce fight, more worthy Hermann's fame,
  Hath crown'd us often with the victor's meeds:
Young eyes have kindled, hearts have felt the flame,
  And burning, thirsted after daring deeds.

BLENHEIM is witness: there, where the dim plains
  In battle thundered; where, with Britons brave
(Worthy as we the blood within their veins),
  The Gaul to hasty flight we Teutons gave.

The work of Genius from the Master's mind
  Is like the hero's deed, which cannot die;
Like that it seeks the crown with laurels twined,
  Manlike deserves, then wears with downcast eye.

TO YOUNG.

Die, hoary seër, die ! Thy branch of palm
Budded long since. To fall with thy last sand
 The tears of joy already stand
 In angels' eyes, so bright and calm !

Still dost thou tarry, when thy monument
Above the clouds is built ? Those midnights fraught
 With holy, earnest, solemn thought,
 The Doubting Spirit with thee spent,

And felt how thy prophetic song, so dread,
Sang to him doomsday, and what Wisdom wills
 When with her mighty voice she fills
 The trumpet that awakes the dead.

Die !   Thou hast taught me that the name of death
Sounds like a triumph which the righteous sing.
 Breathe on me, when thy soul takes wing,
 Thy spirit with departing breath !

THE TWO MUSES.

I saw—oh ! saw I what the present views ?
Saw I the future?—for, with eager soul,
I saw the German with the British Muse
    Flying impetuous to the goal.

Two goals before me did the prospect close,
And crown'd the race: the oaks o'ershadow'd one
With their deep verdure : round the other rose
    Tall palms beneath the evening sun.

Used to the strife, the Muse of Albion stept
Proud to the lists : as on the burning sand
With the Mæonian once, and her who kept
    The Capitol, she took her stand.

H

Her younger rival panted as she came,
Yet panted manly ; and a crimson hue
Kindled upon her cheek a noble flame ;
    Her golden hair behind her flew.

She strove with labouring bosom to contain
Her breath, and leant her forward to the prize.
The herald raised his trumpet, and the plain
    Swam like a dream before her eyes.

Proud of the bold One, of herself more proud,
The Briton with her noble glance regards
Thee, Tuisconè : " Ha ! in that oak-wood
    I grew with thee among the Bards,

But the fame reach'd me, that thou wert no more !
O Muse, who livest while the ages roll,
Forgive me that I learnt it not before :
    Now will I learn it at the goal !

It stands before us.   But the farther crown
Seest thou beyond ? That courage self-possess'd,
That silence proud, and fiery look cast down,
    I know the meaning they confess'd.

Yet weigh the hazard ere the herald sound !
Was I not her competitor who fills
Thermopylæ with song ? and hers renown'd
    Who reigns upon the Seven Hills ?"

She spake. The moment of decision stern
Came with the herald. And with eyes of fire,
" I love thee," quick Teutona did return ;
    " I love thee, Briton, and admire :

But yet not more than immortality,
And those fair palms ! Reach, if thy genius lead,
Reach them before me ! but when thou dost, I
    Will snatch with thee the garland meed.

And—how my heart against its barrier knocks ! —
Perchance I shall be first to gain the wreath ;
Shall feel behind me on my streaming locks
    The fervour of thy panting breath."

The herald sounds : they flew with eagle flight ;
Behind them into clouds the dust was toss'd.
I look'd ; but when the oaks were pass'd, my sight
    In dimness of the dust was lost.

TO CISLY.

INSCRUTABLE beyond the things of earth,
　　That baffle most and mock the wise,
Is heart-felt love ; which springs from real worth,
　　Not from the poet's dream that dies :
A joy ecstatic, which rewards his pain,
　　When comes the hour, almost too blest,
Which tells him,—loving, he is loved again,
　　And those two souls in tranquil rest
Feel better life, and for the first time see
　　Themselves so happy, so alike.
How in that likeness happy ! Who is he,
　　That can with words his feeling speak,
Can speak with tears, or with that look replete
　　With the soul's fulness and its power ?
The sadness that announced it, e'en, is sweet,
　　Ere yet arrived the blissful hour.

If in that sadness one did fruitless grieve,

   Oh! then the spirit falsely chose,

Yet worthily. No thinker can unweave

   The web of those delusive woes.

E'en he that felt them cannot fully sound

   Their depths, though somewhat he discern.

He hears their voice: " Since thou wert worthy found

   To love, that love we bade thee learn.

Now that the magic mystery thou hast known,

   Be follower of the wise, and put

Knowledge in action : for to know alone

   Brings forth to none celestial fruit."

So I obeyed. The vale, like Eden fair,

   CISLY, and in the vale the spring

Delays thee. And, around, the balmy air

   Waves soft its odour-bearing wing.

The rosebuds open to thee now, and breathe

   Their perfume round thy calm repose.

Wake ! for I lightly throw on thee the wreath ;

   Wake at the dewy-sprinkling rose !

My heart long quailed its heavy load beneath ;

   Wake up, and smile away its woes !

THE ROSE-WREATH.

I FOUND her by the shady rill;
  I bound her with a wreath of rose:
She felt it not, but slumber'd still.

I looked on her; and on the spot
  My life with hers did blend and close:
I felt it, but I knew it not.

Some lisping, broken words I spoke,
  And rustled light the wreath of rose:
Then from her slumber she awoke.

She looked on me; and from that hour
  Her life with mine did blend and close;
And round us it was Eden's bower.

TO HER.

O TIME, with dearest blessings fraught,
Near, happy Time, through distant years
    Thee with sad heart I sought,
    And shed too many tears.

Thou comest wafted from above
By angels that were men before,
    Who loved like us, and love
    Like spirits evermore.

On wings of peace and morning air,
With dews of heavenly day bestrown,
    A spring for ever fair,
    To earth thou comest down.

For the soul feels its life, and flows
Through all the heart to rapture moved,
When full of love it knows
The bliss to be beloved.

HER SLUMBER.

She sleeps. Wave round her, Slumber, thy soft wing,
With balmy life her gentle heart imbue :
    From Eden's clear, untroubled spring,
    Bring the light drop of crystal dew.

And let it fall her languid cheek above,
Where the rose dies. And thou, diviner guest,
    The Peace of Virtue and of Love,
    With folded wings o'ershade her rest.

How calm and motionless is her repose !
E'en thou, my lyre, be hushed in silence deep !
    The wreath would wither on my brows,
    If thou should'st whisper her from sleep.

TO GLEIM.

HE knows not mirth, no grace hath he
   Seen smile, who never comprehends,
How favourites of Euphrosyne
   Laugh only with Socratic friends.

Thou knowest it, who lov'st at eve
   To lend light wings to twilight hours,
The duties of the day relieve,
   And wisdom's pathway strew with flowers.

Let the loud laugh thy song profane.
   They feel its charm who know thee best;
And many a Lesbian maid's disdain
   Chastises the profaner's jest.

She smiles not, when the simpering clown
   The tale too lit'rally explains,
But, conscious, bids him with a frown
   Interpret, like her smiles, thy strains.

So learns he what she better knows;
   But though her countenance is bright,
Though at thy song her bosom glows,
   GLEIM's fiery heart she knows not quite.—

His thirst a friend of friends to prove,
   So nobly proud of honour's bays,
Worn by the man that wins his love,
   And hurt by coldness of half praise.

Loving and loved—herein alone
   He hates the mean of moderation,
Or when to Frederic's[1] renown
   His lips let fall their inspiration.

[1] Frederic the Great.

No recompense he sought, nor found.
　Thy strain, though wrong, was nobly free :
But know, O GLEIM, on German ground
　The muse bends not her neck to thee.

In hasty flight to gain the wood
　Where bards reclined in oaken shade,
Thence to the goal that loftier stood
　Amid the palms that never fade,

She sang to me in wrath. My lyre
　Fell to the earth,—fell ringing down.
I saw the priestess' eyes of fire,
　Her streaming hair, and threatening frown.

" Learn from the inmost grove, and bear
　To sons of genius our award.
Else will I seize thy lyre, and tear
　Its strings, and look on thee abhorr'd.

More to us Frederic might have been
　Than liberty's most favour'd foe,
Octavian ; more than time has seen
　In Louis, left so long below.

Such promise gave in youthful age
　　His soul sublime. E'en when the blood
Dripped from his laurels, and the sage
　　In mail of iron armour stood,

The fount of Poesy arose
　　To wash away the sanguine blot;
But turn'd, and through the oak-wood flows,
　　Where Henry's minstrel [2] follows not.

Tell not posterity his fall!
　　How his own worth he scorn'd in pride!
Or tell it sad at heart, and call
　　Your sons his judgment to decide!"

[2] VOLTAIRE, the friend of Frederic the Great, and singer of
Henry IVth. Frederic himself wrote French poetry.

THE FEAR OF MY BELOVED.

Cisly, thou weepest, and I sleep in peace,
Where in the sand the broken road-tracks cease ;
Though dark above the shades of night increase,
  Peaceful I sleep.

Where the road ends the sea is but a tide,
A gently swelling stream o'er which I glide :
For God who leads me bids the wave subside.
  Cisly, why weep ?

THE RHINE-WINE.

Son of the grape, that glitterest in the bowl,
Call to the bower my friend, and none beside.
We three are worthy this age, and that old,
    Good German time, when thou, our pride,

Didst hang unpress'd, but full of fiery blood,
Over the Rhine ; which nurtured thy young stock,
And, careful, cooled with its cerulean flood,
    The foot of thy too burning rock.

Now thy stock bears well-nigh its hundredth year,
'Tis fitting we should learn thy lofty soul
To understand ; and, Cato-like severe,
    Stern virtue kindle at thy bowl.

The teacher of the schools the spirit knows
Of beast and every plant. The poet's eyne
Pierce not so deep : but of the virgin rose
  The weaker spirit, of the wine

The stronger, which she crowns ; and Philomel's
Impassion'd soul, who sits in shade aloof,
And sings to him the vine, he better tells
  Than lips that drop down cause and proof.

By noblest proof, O Rhine-wine, thou canst shew
A worthy son thou art of German ground ;
Glowing, but not inebriating, thou,
  Free from light froth, and strong, and sound.

Thou breathest balm, as when the evening gales
Waft their rich odours from the spicy strand,
Which e'en the trader lingeringly inhales,
  And pushes slowly from the land.

Shut to, my friend, the garden-gate ; for fear
Some crafty man, who scents the aroma's steam,
Pay us unwelcome visit, seat him here,
  Nor speak the words the wise beseem.

Now we are safe. Severer wisdom teach,
And fancies bright, thou soul of Ancient Wine !
Banish not cares. If thee dear sorrows reach,
    Thy cherish'd sorrows shall be mine.

I weep with thee when thou hast lost a friend.
Name him. From me a friend was snatch'd away :
So much he said, when, gasping to his end,
    Came the last pause, and dead he lay !

Of all the griefs that overwhelm our lot,
Till smitten to the ground we nerveless lie,
A friend's death were the greatest, were it not,
    That she, the loved one, too, must die !

But if thy manhood other cares inflame,
And thou dost burn, that with the bardic throng
Not yet the grove thou enterest, and thy name
    Rolls with the stream unmark'd along ;

Bethink thee — Wisdom on the love of Fame
Follows and overtakes it. Folly dwells
In souls that run with an ignoble aim,
    Lured by the tinkling of light bells.

I

Desert still waits thee.   Nobly fill thy part,
The world will know it.   And the part most fair
Is virtue.   To the master-works of Art
     Fame is secure ; to Virtue, rare.

But Immortality beneath the skies
She can forego.   Breathe free, and pledge me, then !
Till the cool breezes of the morn arise,
     Hold we much converse of great men.

FOR THE KING.

Sing, silver-toned Psaltery! pour
   High praise to God, and to thy voice
   Gather the feelings that rejoice
The Lord Jehovah to adore.

Glorious and Merciful, in grace
   Thou gavest to this happy land
   A ruler to bear wise command,
And be the glory of our race.

High thanks to the Great Giver rise!
   Hail to the king whom God has given!
   Look down and bless, O Lord of heaven,
Look down with unaverted eyes!

Look down, and grant him length of days !
   Grant, Thou that lovest those that love,
   Calm days and peaceful from above
To the good king, whom nations praise ;—

Him whom we love, our soul's delight :
   For whom the tears of gladness flow !
   Peace to thee ! To the conqueror woe,
Who treads the field of bloody fight,

Where not the war-steeds rage more fierce
   Than foams the hero for renown.
   Die ! though thick laurels shade thy crown,
Beneath—the Thunderer's eyes shall pierce.

Curses pursue thee.   Loud acclaim
   Blesses the prince whose noble scorn
   Glory contemns of Misery born,
Ambitious of a better fame.

He speaks from where the summits rise,
   " Thou know'st, Renown, but outward deeds."
   Noble, he seeks not Virtue's meeds
E'en in the applauses of the wise.

A conscience pure,—that is the best,
   The loftiest good, the wise assays,
   The wiser gains. Not angel's praise
Can make a king supremely blest,

Who consecrates to God his days.
   At early dawn the babe's sweet lips
   Lisp with Thy name : when the sun dips
Behind the hills, for Thee he prays.

I saw the wise man die in faith,
   A Christian in this pagan age.
   And thus with looks of love the sage
His grandson charged with parting breath :—

" My first and ceaseless thanks be given
   To God, who did my soul create,
   And calls it from this mortal state
Up to the eternal life of heaven.

And then, with adoration deep,
   I praise him for that heaven-sent friend !
   Bless him, O God : O God defend !
Turn not away, my son, to weep !

God bless him ! this alone can pour
   The drop of wormwood in my cup,
   That my dim eye in vain looks up
To see my king beloved once more.

Long time shalt thou, my happier son,
   Behold him, till hoar age prepare
   For him the crown of silver hair,
And honours of a course well run.

What joy to feel he lived alone
   To God, and see around him stand
   His righteous deeds, a glorious band,
That follow to the judgment throne.

Much have I seen, the fairest, best
   Of human life.   That is to me
   The noblest sight man's eye can see —
A king who makes his people blest.

His favour be thy noble pride.
   Seek modest worth : he bids it spring ;
   And now once more, God bless the king !
The best of kings." And so he died.

CONVALESCENCE.

MILD Convalescence, daughter fair
Of Nature, not of Immortality,
Down from the Lord of life and death to me
    Thee wingèd angels bear.

Had I not heard thy light-drawn breath,
Thy gentle footfall and thy whispers low,
Then had been furrow'd on my still cold brow
    The iron foot of death.

True, I had soar'd through azure skies,
Where circling worlds round other suns return ;
Had trod the track where sweeping comets burn,
    Lost to our failing eyes :

Had greeted with admiring gaze
The dwellers in those earths and in those suns,
And life that breathes in myriad forms, nor shuns
    The comet's mist and blaze :

Had ask'd my youthful questions bold,
And heard full answers I could understand ;
Learnt more in hours than here the weary sand
    Of ages can unfold.

But then—oh, I had left undone
What in the blossom of my days high Choice
Already call'd me with her clear sweet voice
    To hold in thought begun.

Mild Convalescence, daughter fair
Of Nature, not of Immortality,
Down from the Lord of life and death to me
    Thee wingèd angels bear.

TO THE OMNIPRESENT.

WHEN Thou with Death didst wrestle and with Hell
 In prayer and agony profound,
When first the blood-sweat fell
 Upon the hallow'd ground,

In that dread hour sublime
 The mighty truth Thou gavest to our trust,
Which shall be truth, till time
 No longer sheathe the living soul in dust.

Then Thou didst stand and speak
 To those on whom deep slumber stole ;
  " All willing is the soul ;
   The flesh is weak."

This lot of finite being, this earth's weight,
     Upon my spirit lies,
When up to God, the Infinite, elate,
     It fain would rise.

I fall adoring in the dust, and weep.
  Receive my tears, the voice of finite love!
Give my soul truer life, that it may keep
  Its soaring flight up to the throne above.

Father, all-present, Thou dost close
     My being round.
Stand still, O Contemplation! and repose
  By this well-spring of thought on holy ground.

What will Thine intuition be when thought
  Hath felt the powers of the world of light?
Wherewith shall be that intuition fraught,
  O Thou, all-present and all-infinite?

No eye hath seen it, and no ear hath heard,
  It came into no heart, howe'er it strove,
Howe'er the thought of God within it stirr'd,
  Howe'er it thirsted after endless love;

It came into no heart of man to say
  (Not into his, who is a sinner spared
A little while on earth, and then dead clay!)
  What God for them that love Him has prepared.

Few—ah! but few are here,
  Whose eye in the created spheres
Sees the Creator: few whose ear
  Him in the rushing of the whirlwind hears:

Or in loud thunder, or the lisping brook,
    Thee, Increate, descries.
Few hearts there are that tremble in the look
    Of God's all-present eyes.

Thee in the Holy Place
  Still let me seek and find!
Thou, who art present through all space,
  Be ever present to my mind!

And if the thought grow dim,
  Let me with tears of joyful awe
Down from the choir of seraphim
    New rapture draw.

Devout, may I prepare
   To see Thy face;
To see Thee there
   In the Most Holy Place!

I raise mine eyes, and look;
   And lo! the Lord does all pervade.
Earth, from whose dust He took
   Wherewith the first of men He made,

Where my first life is pass'd,
   Where I must soon decay,
Then rise again at last—
   God deigns to thee His presence, too, for aye!

I pluck with holy hand
   The flower that decks the sod.
It sprang at God's command,
   And where the flower is, is God.

I feel with holy awe the rising breeze,—
   I hear its moan.   God bids it moan and rise.
   And He is there both where it sighs,
And where the thunder breaks the cedar-trees.

Rejoice, O Flesh, to be Death's heir!
  When thou shalt moulder with the clod,
    He will be there,
      The Eternal God!

Rejoice to be Death's heir. Thy dust shall flee
  To Depth and Height, and waste itself in air.
But where those wasted atoms fall will He
  The Eternal God be there.

The heights, the depths, shall fain
  Bow to the word of Fate,
When the All-Present One again
  From dust immortals shall create.

Cast down your palms and crowns! adore ye
  The Giver of your breath.
  Shout Hallelujah to the King of Death,
    To the Creator glory!

Mine eye looks up, and sees,
  And lo! the Lord is every where.
Ye suns, and earths, and moons, encircling these,
  The presence of the All-Present ye declare!

Night of the worlds, as Him we darkly see
  In the mysterious Word,
So in the depths of thine obscurity
    Seek we the Lord.

Here stand I—Earth! What is this mortal frame
  To the unnumber'd worlds that round me roll?
Those countless worlds, which angels cannot name,
  What are they to my soul?

To the immortal and redeemèd soul
  Nearer Thou art than to those worlds afar.
For they know not, they feel not, as they roll
  Thy Presence where they are.

I muse thereon, and tell
  To Thee my thanks, Thou Ever-near!
With tears of joy, with bliss unspeakable,
  Father, I thank Thee, when I feel Thee here.

Moments of mercy Thou dost shower,
  When that angelic sense supreme
Of thine all-present power
  Upon my soul Thou biddest stream.

But one such moment spent
  With Thee, eternal Sire,
  Is like an age entire
    Of full content.

E'en as my spirit burns
  To reach the hour when dust shall live again,
So my soul yearns
  Those moments of Thy mercy to obtain.

Prostrate I lie before Thee, O my trust!
  I would lie lower, child of sinful birth,
Bow'd in the dust,
  The nethermost of lowest earth!

Now canst thou think and feel?
  From dust thou shalt arise,
And higher think and happier feel,
  And see thy God with unbeclouded eyes.

But, O my soul, through whom
  Shalt thou His glory see?
Through Him, O ransom'd from the tomb,
  Who was, who is, and who shall be!

Thou, whom no words can name,

   Reveal Thy presence to the spirit's eye.

Give every thought a noble aim,

   And point it to the sky.

    Thy present Deity

   My every sense inspire ;

   And send me wings of fire,

And lead me, Increate, to Thee !

What am I, dying worm ?

   And what art Thou, Divine ?

Strengthen, establish me, confirm,

   That I may evermore be Thine.

Thine could I *not* be without Him,

   My teacher, who for me did bleed and groan ;

Without whom, Thine all-presence were a dim,

   Dread feeling of omnipotence unknown.

When heaven and earth have pass'd,

   Thy promises, O Son, abide.

From the first fallen to the last

   Redeem'd by Him who died,

Whom the archangel's trumpet-tone
   Shall call from death a better life to see;
Thou hast been ever with thine own,
   Thou with thine own wilt ever be.

My finger felt not where the nails had gored;
     My hand I never laid
   In the deep wound the spear-head made;
Yet thou art mine, my God and Lord!

THE INTUITION OF GOD.

WITH trembling I rejoice
　　Nor dare the truth believe,
Were not the voucher's voice
The voice of God who knows not to deceive.

　　For well I know and feel
　　　I am but sinful clay;
　　Should know and feel it well,
　　　E'en if to me diviner day

　　Had not set all my sins in clearer light,
　　　And, rending guilt's dark-mantling stole,
　　Uncover'd to my wiser sight
　　　The fashion of my wounded soul.

With lowly-bended knee,
  With hands that deep adoring fold,
I taste the joyful mystery,
  That God I shall behold.

I search into that thought divine,
  Which thou art equal, soul, to think :
Who drawing nearer the grave's brink
  Know'st that eternal life is thine.

Not that thou darest go
  Into the Holy, Holy Place to gaze.
There many a gift is treasured, that below
  Unheeded waked no gratitude and praise.

Only from far one mild and gentle beam,
    Lest my soul die,
One mild and cloud-attemper'd gleam
    Of glory meets my eye.

How great was he who dared to pray,
  " If I have found Thy favour, Lord,
Let me Thy glory see to-day ! "
  So to the Eternal pray'd he, and was heard.

The land of Golgotha he never trod :
    An earlier death avenged his crime,
In that he once — but once — mistrusted God.
    How in his chastisement he stands sublime !

The Father hid him in the hollow rock,
    When the Son pass'd in glory where he stood ;
Then paused the trump on Sinai's top, nor broke
    The voice of thunder, when God spake of God.

Now, in no shroud of night,—
    In that day's light
Which casts no shadow, morn nor e'en,
For ages long (so deem we) he hath seen

Beyond the bounds of Time, serene,
    Nor conscious of fleet moments that record
Their flight to moments — he hath seen
    Thy glory, Holy, Holy, Holy Lord !

    Joy deep and inexpress'd,
Thought of that vision to the righteous given,
Thou art the hope on which I rest,
    The rock on which I stand, and gaze to heaven.

When sin-born fear
 When Death's dark frown,
Threatening and near,
 Would cast me down,

  Upon this rock-built tower,
 O Thou, whom now the righteous dead behold,
Let me stand firm, when Death's o'erwhelming pow'r
 His shroud of darkness doth around me fold.

Rise, O my soul, above mortality!
 Look up, and see with wondering eyne
The Father's bright effulgency
 Beaming in Jesus' face divine.

Hosanna, yea, Hosanna! Godhead dwells
 With Christ the man, that sits on Zion's hill;
The cherub's quivering harp-tone scarcely swells,
 Its note scarce sounds, but trembles, and is still.

Hosanna, yea, Hosanna, sing!
 For Godhead now is one
With Christ the King,
 With Jesus, Mary's son.

When e'en that forecast beam of light,
 That prophecy of blood shone clear on earth,
And more His form with sorrow and despite
 Was marr'd than any man's of mortal birth;

When men regarded not,—the rather
 The cherubim look'd down,
And saw the glory of the Father
 In the countenance of the Son.

 I see the witness there.
Through seven nights he watch'd the morrow
In doubt and wonder, and with sorrow
 Wrestled in prayer.

 I see him pray.
His risen Lord before him stands.
He lays his finger in His wounded hands,
 And earth and heaven pass away!

He sees the Father's glory in the Son.
 I hear his voice aloud.
He sees not heaven or earth: he sees but ONE,
 And cries, My Lord! my God!

THE SPRING FESTIVAL.

INTO the sea of worlds I will not soar,
  Nor launch me where in radiance bright
Creation's first-born sons in choirs adore,
  Till their songs fail for rapture of delight.

But only by one drop that fell below,
  Only by Earth, adoring, will I stand.
Praise ye the Lord ! the drop that did o'erflow
  Ran down from the Almighty's hand.

When flow'd forth from that hand of might
The greater worlds, and rushing streams of light
Form'd seven stars, each a resplendent crown ;
From the same hand, O drop, thou rannest down.

When from one stream of light our sun arose,
  And when a flood, rushing as from the top
Of mountain-rocks, Orion did enclose ;
  From the same hand thou rannest down, O drop !

What are the myriad and the myriad births
  That people thee and peopled ? What am I ?
More—praise my Maker—than those rolling earths,
  More than those seven stars that stream'd on high.

But thou, poor insect of the May,
  That sportest near me in thy green and gold,
Thou livest, but thy form perchance for aye
    Death shall enfold.

I walk'd abroad to worship, and I weep !
  O Thou, the tears forgive,
That fall o'er those that sleep an endless sleep,
  Thou who dost ever live !

All doubt Thou wilt extinguish, when
  Thou lead'st me through the vale of death and dole.
Emerging from that darkness I shall ken
  Whether the golden insect have a soul.

If thou art fashion'd but of dust,
   Son of the May, be dust again !
The playmate of each fickle gust,
   Or whatsoe'er the Eternal may ordain !

Pour forth anew, mine eye,
   Thy blissful shower !
And thou, my harp, reply,
   And praise the God of power !

With palms my harp is crown'd
   To sing my true delight !
I stand, and look around,
   And all is marvel, all is might !

I look upon the world with deeper awe.
     From Thee,
   Mysterious Deity,
Being it took, and law.

Ye airs that float around me, and your balm,
   Breathe cool upon my glowing brow,
You, wondrous in your might and in your calm,
   The Lord, the Infinite, bade flow.

But now ye languish, now ye scarcely breathe,
    Sultry looks down the morning sun.
The gathering clouds together wreathe,
    And visibly He comes—the Eternal One!

How the winds rise, and roar, and whirl around!
    How the stream swells, and the tall forests nod!
Clear as may shine on eyes with darkness bound,
    All visible Thou art, Eternal God!

The forest bows, the torrent flows,—and I
      Fall not upon my face?
O Lord, my God, whose mercy is so nigh,
    Look on me with Thy pitying grace!

Lord, is Thine anger hot,
    Because with darkness Thou art clad?
    The darkness makes the furrows glad:
Father, Thine anger burneth not.

The genial shower is gushing
    On the blade and grassy plot,
On grape-bunches, heart-refreshing—
    Father, Thine anger burneth not.

All, all is still, where Thou art nigh ;
 Stillness is all around.
 E'en the gold insect pauses on the ground.
Hath it, perchance, a soul, and will not die ?

Oh, that my soul could praise Thee as it thirsts !
 More glorious now I see Thy form ;
 Darker around Thee swells the storm,
Then full of blessing bursts.

See ye the signs around Him pour'd ?
 Beneath His step the lightnings flash ?
 Hear ye Jehovah's thunder-crash,
The shivering thunder of the Lord ?

 O God, the Lord,
Compassionate and full of grace,
Be Thy great name adored
 And magnified in every place.

What of the stormy winds ?   They bring the thunders,
 And revel in the forest, roaring loud.—
Now all is still ; and slowly wanders
 The dark retiring cloud.

See ye the vivid lightnings that pass over ?
   Hear ye the peals that herald the Supreme ?
The thunders shout aloud, Jehovah !
   The crashing oak-woods steam.

Not so our hut of clay.
   Our Father with a smile of peace
   Bade the destroying angel cease,
And from our cottage turn away.

Now heaven and earth resound
   With gushing rains in overflowing measure.
Soft they refresh the thirsty ground,
   And heaven unburden of her treasure.

And, lo ! no more in storm and thunder,
   But in soft breezes whispering low
     Jehovah comes ; and under
   His footstep bends the peaceful bow.

THE COMPASSIONATE.

A MARVEL to admire
  Is my soul's bliss !
Nay to a nobler thought aspire :
  To marvel only is to praise amiss.

Amazement, wing thy heavenward flight,
  Adoring the Eternal Sire !
Thou, rapture of supreme delight,
  Stream on my soul your holy fire !

And fill with blessedness
  My overflowing frame,
Till oft the spirit's rapt excess
  Break forth in flame !

Thou art eternal ! What can thought avail ?
  My soul stands still, nor knows Thee as Thou art.
O Father, Father, so my thoughts must fail,
  So my lips stammer, and so feel my heart !

      The Sire above
Fall down and worship, all ye heavenly powers !
  For He whose name is Love
Your Father is, and ours.

Ye who shall erst with seraphim rejoice
      And wondering praise,
  Go, and search through this Eden maze,
Where speaks Jehovah's voice.

It speaks in thunder, in the wingèd storm,
  In the soft sighing of the breeze.
But clearer, longer, in the form
  Of speech, as once among the garden trees.

The thunder dies, the storm departs, the winds
  Sink into stillness : but the living word
Streams with the ages, and each moment finds
  The fuller utterance of the Lord.

Am I still earthly ? or beyond the grave ?
  The heavenward flight have I already soar'd ?—
O word, so strong to save,
    Thus saith the Lord.

" Her suckling can the mother's heart forget,
  And feel no pity for its tender moan ?
Perchance she may : and yet
  I never will forget mine own."

Praise, adoration, tears that start
  In glad and grateful eyes,
Warm thanks, that well from a full heart,
  For immortality arise !

Sing Hallelujah in the Holy Place,
  And then within the veil,
Sing Hallelujah there before His face,
  Who spake the word that cannot fail.

Lie low in deep amaze,
  My soul, who liv'st for aye.
Drink the full blessing, and Jehovah praise
  Who spake the word, that cannot pass away.

UNIVERSAL BLESSEDNESS.

My hand upon my mouth I laid,
  And silent stood before the Lord :
Then took my fallen harp, and bade
  To God, to God, resound the chord.

When in the earth the seed is sown
  To ripen for the day of sheaves,
When planted in the heavens my soul is grown
  A cedar of my God with outspread leaves,

  When I at length am taught
  As I was known to know,
And — mount my soul to the exalting thought !—
  To love as I was loved below,—

To love as I was loved
    By God himself,—by God !
Ah ! then !—But here, so far removed,
    How can I feel it in this earthly clod ?

What is it stirs within me, that I thirst
    With life so bounded by a narrow line
The limits of my prison-house to burst ?
    'Tis that I know a nobler life is mine.

How glorious are Thy thoughts, O God, to me !
    How numberless ! Should I their tale divine.
More are they than the sand by the salt sea !
    And one is — that a nobler life is mine.

O hope, that soarest to the skies,
    The foretaste of a life sublime,
Already dost thou bid my spirit rise
    Above the finite bounds of time.

Thou art the longing of my weary heart,
    Thou art its thirst, my King and God !
I will extol Thee, glorious as Thou art,
    Thy glorious name for evermore will laud.

L

Whence was His birth, and where is He,
  Worthy, like Godhead, of my love?
Oh! none is found throughout mortality,
  None in the worlds above.

Fountain of life, salvation's living well,
  From Thee what blessing flow'd,
  For them who kept their high abode,
And for the souls that fell.

That thousand-armèd stream descends below
  Through all the labyrinth of human life,
  With blessings upon blessings rife,
Whose well-spring once was woe.

O Woe, thou pillar planted in the sand,
  With Joy's unnumber'd garlands crown'd,
Thou reachest upward to a better land,
  Where the eternal river flows around.

Thou art the Father of all spirits,
  O God; through Thee they were.
And each through Thee inherits
  The heritage of glory's heir.

What endless generations ! Though my soul
  Through long millenniums riper grow,
How small a part of the created whole,
  How few of my coævals, I shall know !

How few of those who worship with me there
  When I my crown beside their crowns shall lay !
O God, my Father, shall I longer dare
  To speak with Thee, who am but fragile clay ?

Forgive, Eternal Sire,
  Forgive the dead of future days
His sins, his vain desire,
  His feeble song of praise.

The life of all that are alive,
  Thou art from everlasting God.
To grasp that thought in vain I strive,
  And sink beneath a whelming flood.

Life of our life, oh joy ! Thou art !
  Else what were I, if Thou wert not ?
Thou wilt be, and to me Thy life impart,
  Spirit of spirits, Ruler of my lot.

First of all spirits Thou,
    Yet different from all ;
But they around Thee, moving to and fro,
    Like shadows of Thy glory fall.

Why, self-sufficing, mad'st Thou any thing ?
    Because to countless blessed sprites
Thou wouldest be the inexhaustive spring
    Of pure delights.

More blessed wert Thou in dispensing bliss ?
    Ah ! here the finite feels its utmost bound.
I can grow dizzy o'er this vast abyss,
    But nothing see in its profound !

O sacred Night ! by thee I stand and think.
    In a far future state
The veil, perchance, shall sink
    That hides the mysteries of Fate.

Knowledge, perchance, shall God create,
    Such as my power, and all the thoughts that glow.
How manifold soe'er they be, and great,
    Such as the whole creation cannot shew.

My future being, how I long to meet thee !
   I feel myself so little among men :
Yet feel I, when thy visions greet me,
   How great I shall be then.

Oh ! hope that mounts on high,
   Oh ! hope that God hath sent ! .
One brief and hasty twinkling of an eye
   (They call it death), and I shall be content !

Already is my spirit sped
   Above the hopes that highest soar'd.
From henceforth blessed are the dead,
   That slumber in the Lord.

Sin's wages are—the moment when we die.
   But from behind that dreaded night,
Through thickset starry openings in the sky,
   Streams down celestial light.

Let but that moment, as a fleeting breath,
   Transport me into truer day ;
O Lord of life and death,
   Take in Thine hour of grace my soul away !

Whether it come with calm and gentle pace,
　　Or like the march of thunder through the skies,
Oh! take this body in Thine hour of grace,
　　And sow it in the earth, where it shall rise!

How my soul's triumph it shall then enhance,
　　When its last lingering look is backward thrown,
To see with that last glance
　　　The seed is duly sown.

How cheering is the thought
　　To him who sees its promise bloom—
With what exulting triumph fraught—
　　" Christ also died and slumber'd in the tomb!"

THE KING'S RECOVERY.

To Him who saved our king glad thanks we raise.
   Thou, Thou alone didst shield his days,
      O Lord of life and doom ;
   Thine be the glory, thanks, and praise,
      Our father's Rescuer from the tomb!

Our thankful tears we offer unto Thee :
   That offering on bended knee
      Low at Thy throne we give,
   Whence issued forth the high decree,
      Let Mine anointed live.

Thy work was wonderful, O God of Fate ;
   Father, Thy mercy was too great,—
      Too great for us to share.
   Up to the Giver mount elate
      Our strong and frequent prayer.

Many succumbed. To him the gentle touch
   Of Thy benignant hand was such
      As brought us no dismay.
   Father, Thy mercy was too much,
      Which spared our hope that day.

He whom we love survives,—and we no less.
   For at what time Thy bounteous grace
      To him did safety give,
   Us did Thy gentle arm embrace :—
      Earth trembled, and we live ! [1]

[1] " A later earthquake than that of Lisbon : it lasted a short time, and was not violent. I heard, however, my pictures rattle against the wall, and the table at which I was sitting was so shaken, that I started up, seized my papers, and was about to escape, when it was already passed."—KLOPSTOCK.

When the ground shook beneath our staggering path,
   Thy voice of mercy, not of wrath,
     Call'd us to look on high,
   Above earth's fading death-mown swathe,
     To Him who cannot die.

E'en yet with awe the tremulous sound I hear.
   The Judge's arm that, raised severe,
     Does other lands appal,
   Till tottering cities quake with fear,
     And thunder, crash, and fall;

Or gives the people to the weltering sword,
   That arm is stretch'd out to accord
     The blessing we partake;
   And to give thanks for that award,
     It gently bids us wake.

Fall on your faces, and with thanks adore!
   All hearts your Hallelujah pour
     To God who rules benign.
   Mercy and truth Thou hast in store,
     Honour and praise be Thine!

Did not His glory pass before our eyes ?
Let us pursue it to the skies ;
And ever on our thought
Let Memory like an echo rise
Of that which God has wrought.

Tell it your children's children ; bid them learn
The deed that claims their heart's return.
No old man meet his end,
Till, ere his lamp yet cease to burn,
His fervid thanks ascend.

Grant us, O Father, this thanksgiving grace.
Let adoration, glory, praise,
Thy mighty name confess.
In heaven Thine arm Thou didst upraise
To bless us, Lord, to bless !

THE WORLDS.

GREAT is the Lord, and great
   Are all his deeds around.
Thou sea of worlds, whose drops are stars,
   Thy depths we cannot sound.

Where shall my tongue begin, or end,
   When it Thy glory sings?
What thunder lends to me its voice?
   My thoughts what angel brings?

Who leads me up on high
   To the eternal hills?
I sink, I sink in boundless space
   Which that world-ocean fills.

How fair the starry vault arose
   Ere my thought dared its bolder flight?
Ere yet it ventured to demand,
   What is His work who rules in light?

Demanded of myself — vain dust!
   I fear'd, when I began to ask,
Lest that should be, what now I find,
   And I succumb beneath the task.

Less venturous than I,
   Such fate the pilot knows,
When he on far Olympus sees
   The gathering tempest close.

The sea sleeps still in awful calm:
   Yet sees he in the west
How fierce a storm shall soon descend,
   And fear invades his breast.

Pallid the swelling sail
   He lashes to the mast.
Ah! now the sea begins to foam,
   The storm is hurrying past!

The sea roars louder than the hills,
  Crashes the mast beneath the surge,
The howling tempest rages loud,
  And sings the dead-men's dirge.

He knows it.   Higher swells the wave,
  The last, that brings the ship its doom :
The dead-men's dirge is howling still
  O'er the storm's vast and yawning tomb.

THE NEW AGE.

Blow soft, ye winds, upon their tomb !
　Or if some arm unconscious where they lay
Did chance the patriots' dust exhume,
　　Oh, waft it not away !

Scorn him, my lyre, who holds their honour light,—
　Scorn, though perchance from hero's blood he spring.
They rescued us from hundred-headed might,
　　And gave to us one king.

O Freedom, to the ear
　A sweet and silv'ry chime ;
Light to the soul, to thought an ampler sphere,
　　A passion in the heart sublime !

O Freedom, not the democrat alone
　Knows what thou art ;
But the good monarch's happy son
　Hath bound thee to his heart.

Not for the land alone
　Where law and hundreds reign,
But for the land—his own—
　To law and one a fair domain,

He, whose great heart deserves the crown,
　Mounts some Thermopylæ on high,
Some lofty altar of renown,
　Where he bedecks himself to die.

Bright immortality be thine !
　Thy hallow'd hair that drips with blood
The Muse with blooming wreaths shall twine,
　And shed for thee a tender flood.

Noble and sweet it is to share [1]
　For Fatherland the soldier's grave :
　For Frederic and his people brave,
The sons of his paternal care.

---

[1] At this period Denmark was in danger of war.

Yonder methought a spirit passed,
  Kindling each patriot warrior band.
Thou flowest, flowest fast,
  O blood, for Fatherland.

Names that fell strange upon our ears,
  Upward, methought, like eagles, sped.
The bride, the mother, dried their tears,
  For tears profaned the glorious dead.

But with more manly wisdom, and a love
  More noble than the warrior's zeal,
He press'd his hand the hilt above,
  When Europe thunder'd Frederic was still.

We give thee thanks, paternal king,
  That we can keep thy feast and ours
Beneath the bounty-laden wing
  Of Peace, in shady bowers.

Not with the pomp and boisterous mirth
  Of joy that does but sound and gleam ;
But, as befits thy noble worth,
  With grateful praise to earth's Supreme.

Who gave us thee and thine, we keep
    Our festival, so calm and dear,
With heartfelt joy, whose well is deep,
    And overflows in many a tear.

Departed Age, that slumberest dumb,
    Lift up thy sunken head once more,
Give to the century to come
    The blessing that was thine before.

He rises from his silent pillow,
    And speaks his blessing : Fred'ric sage
And Christian, meet his steps to follow,
    Alone shall bless the dawning age.

We and our children supplicate
    The Providence, that now appears
So watchful o'er the people's fate,
    To rule their coming years.

Heard ye that ruler's thundering scale
    Sound with its dreadful clang,
And cries arose of blood and wail,
    Of peace few echoes rang !

M

The thund'ring balance rings, and weighs ;
　　One grain cast in by Fate and Time
This scale and that alternate sways
　　To victories of blood and crime.

And thus shall speak the warrior's lips ;
　　Not the fierce death of stormy fight,
But that dread beam that mounts and dips,
　　And its death-tones my soul affright.

O Providence, the strife conclude !
　　Bid the bloody victory cease !
And be again subdued
　　By the victory of peace !

So shall our Father keep, and we,—
　　He for the love he bears his own,
　　We for the love we bear the throne,—
Unbroken our festivity.

How happy is our lot !
　　Blow soft, ye winds, the patriot's bones above :
They, too, are unforgot
　　And share in Fred'ric's love.

O joyous year, of a new age prime-born,
  Smiling with hope so glad and gay ;
On rosy pinions of the summer morn
  Thou risest to the perfect day.

THE CONSTELLATIONS.

FIELD and forest tell His glory, vale and mountain-rock,
And the shore resounds in thunder to the surging ocean-shock.
Praise they give to the Eternal when the billows roll,
But the thankful song of Nature cannot utter forth the whole.

Yet she sings to her Creator an exalted strain :
Down from heaven swells the echo, ringing through the world again
And the lightning's storm-mate, underneath the cloudy night,
Calls aloud from mountain-peak and each crashing pine-clad height

In the grove the branches wave, the brooklet, babbling, strays ;
And they keep all day together their glad festival of praise ;
And the gentle breezes waft it to the bow of space,
Where in clouds it stands aloft, pledge of safety and of grace.

And art *thou* then silent ? thou whom God eternal made ?
Art thou dumb amid the praises rising up from sun and shade ?
Thee he gave immortal being ! glad His praise prolong,
Though He lives beyond the reach of the soaring of thy song.

Drinking of the stream, adore the Giver and the source.
Glittering choir of constellations, moving round in glorious course.
Ye extol the Everlasting ! I, below, would fain aspire
To blend with your eternal chorus raptures of my earthly lyre.

Who the worlds created—there that sinking golden sea,
Here the dust with living creatures myriad-teeming—who is He ?
God he is, our Father, for we dare to name Him thus.
Countless voices from all creatures celebrate that name with us.

He the worlds created :—there the Lion's fiery heart,
There the Ram, the Capricorn, the Seven Pleiades apart,
And the Scorpion, and the Crab, and forms that higher tread ;
There the Archer points his arrow, and the lightning shaft is sped.

How the arrows, when he turns him, in the quiver ring !
How the Twins united shine, in their glory triumphing,
As they march along the heavens scattering light below !
And the Fish, in space disporting, blows forth glittering streams
    that glow.

In the wreath the Rose is fragrant with the dews of light,
And the flame-eyed Eagle soaring vindicates imperial right
O'er his bright companions.   Bending proud his neck so slim,
See the Swan with wing upraised slowly through the azure swim!

Starry Lyre, who gave thee thy melodious tone divine?
And the everlasting strings did with lustrous gold entwine?
Thou resoundest through the dance of planets as they trace
To thy music courses round thee, cycling through the rings of space.

Sweeping by in gay apparel, there the Virgin shines,
With the wheat-ears in her hand and the foliage of the vines.
From the Urn leaps forth the light : see Orion turn,
Looking on the starry girdle ; for he looks not on the Urn.

Oh ! if God upon the Altar should pour out the Bowl,
All creation would be shiver'd into wrecks beneath the pole :
The Lion's heart be broken, and the fallen Urn be dry ;
The Wreath would wither, and the Lyre resound the death-note
        through the sky !

Yonder their Creator made them : nearer to this earth the moon.
Gleaming through the cooler night, serene contentment is her boon ;
Quiet to the toil-worn—in that night when mortals sleep,
And the stars around them shining their eternal courses keep.

Him I praise, the Lord, the Maker, who commandment gave
To the cooler night, so sacred, of the moon and of the grave,
To be light in darkness.   Earth that art our destined tomb.
Waiting daily to receive us, God has strewn thy fields with bloo

New-creating, when at length he takes the judgment-throne.
He shall stir the bone-fill'd grave, and the fields where seed is sow:
He who sleeps shall wake.   The thunder of the trumpet's breat
Calls to judgment ; and is heard and answer'd by the grave and
                    death.

TO THE INFINITE.

How the heart rises when it contemplates
   Thee, the Eternal ! and how low
It sinks when on itself it meditates,
   And, wailing, sees but darkness, death, and woe.

Thou from that darkness callest me,—true aid
   In woe and death.   Thou bad'st me ever live.
I feel it, glorious God ; nor in the shade
   Of death, nor in high heaven, due thanks and praise can give.

Wave, trees of life, into melodious song !
   Flow forth in heavenly music, crystal stream !
Ye may not, as ye murmur soft along,
   Tell all His praise : for God ye sing Supreme !

Thunder in trumpet-tones, ye worlds afar !
　Thou, great Orion, thou, celestial Lyre,
Sound in your glittering courses, every star,
　To swell your trumpet-choir !

O worlds, your thunder loud,
　Your trumpet-choir in vain assays
To tell the whole ! For God,
　God is it, whom ye praise !

DEATH.

Ye starry hosts that glitter in the sky,
　How ye exalt me!　Trancing is the sight
Of all thy glorious works, Most High!
　How lofty art thou, all-creating sprite!

What joy to gaze upon those hosts, to one
　Who feels himself so little, God so great!
Himself but dust, and the great God his own!
　Oh! when I die, such rapture on me wait!

Why art thou dreadful, Death?—the tired man's sleep!
　Oh! cloud not o'er my heavenly delight!
I sink to earth a seed that God shall keep:
　The deathless shall illusive death affright?

Go down then to corruption, mortal form!

    Into that vale the fallen all descend.

Go to the hosts that shelter'd from the storm

        Sleep to the end!

AGANIPPE AND PHIALA,

(THE FOUNTAIN OF MOUNT HELICON AND THE SOURCE OF
THE JORDAN.)

INTO the upper vale the Rhine comes down
Roaring amain, as if the rocks and woods
  Came with it ; and its stream rolls on
  As when the swollen ocean floods

Break thundering on the shore : the river sweeps
Foaming along, and with tumultuous brawl
  Into the valley sprays and leaps,
  And turns to silver in the fall.

So flows, TUISCO, so resounds the song
Of thy true Bards.   In slumber's torpid spell,
  O, Father, deep it lay and long,
  Deaf to the harp-tone's fall and swell

Struck by Apollo in Hellenic clime,
When to Eurotas and her laurel shade
    He woke his minstrelsy sublime
    In measures that high Nature bade ;

And taught the stream and taught the grove his strain
The river roll'd sonorously below,
    The laurels breathed a soft refrain,
    And echo'd back Eurotas' flow.

Tuisco's child waked not from iron sleep,—
From iron sleep, absorb'd in dreams profound.
    But louder from the palm-clad steep,
    By Phiala on holy ground.

The Prophets' lofty song arose.   With joy
Stammering he heard it.   Long ago inspired
    The mother sang it to the boy,
    And the youth marvell'd and admired.

Loud by the sedges of the coral sea
It thunder'd : on Gerizim : by the brook
    Of Kison.   And, Moriah, thee
    The psalm and the hosanna shook,

From the vine-hill the Shulamite in pity
Pour'd loud lament above the fane that lay
   In ruins, and bewail'd the city
   Shrouded in horror and dismay.

THE BLESSED.

THEE only to admire
  How it exalts the spirit of this frame !
The thought of God is as a fire
  That burns within, and feeds a heavenward flame.

Can mortal man be bless'd ?
  Is bliss the boon of travellers to the grave ?
Speak, ye who know that heavenly guest,
  Is it the name ye not unworthy gave,

E'en in the dust, e'en here,
  To that glad sense of His all-perfect being,
Which God bestows, when joyous fear
  Is yours,—as in a dream the Almighty seeing,

Translated ere ye die ?

   Flee to far worlds, and be the friend of those
Who see a past eternity
   Of thought and action : there is thy repose !

Alone the vision of the Lord
   Can to thy soul that bliss unfold ;
That sense of perfectness afford
   When thou with joyous fear shalt God behold !

THE EMPEROUR HENRY.

LET sleep our princes on their velvet throne,
'Mid fumes of courtiers' incense unrenown'd !
Then in their cold and narrow bed of stone
    Sink to oblivion more profound !

Ask not the sculptur'd tomb, Who sleeps beneath ?
O'er names unknown it utters golden praise.
Beside these graves, so barren of a wreath,
    The curious herald wond'ring stays.

So let them slumber on !   And e'en such fate
On him attends, who where the battle bled
Won his victorious way ; but too elate
    If he the Gallic Pindus tread.[1]

[1] Frederic the Great.

By him unheard the oak-woods spread aloft,
And swell sonorous o'er the German fount,
And waft to heaven their song.   An alien scoff'd,
    He climbs not e'en the Gallic mount!

Swift stream and torrent swift, two fountains leap
Forth from the oak in umbrage of the palm ;
Ye see the sister-fountains pure and deep,
    See the bard's Tempè breathing balm.

Depart, Unhallowed!   From thy troubled gaze
Veil'd Beauty stands for evermore conceal'd.
No longer at its rock the fountain plays,
    But rushes through the wold and weald.

What spirits wander from the deeper grove ?
Leave ye the vale of death and hither throng,
O Heroes, where your later children rove,
    To hear our self-avenging song?

For ah! too long we linger'd !   But to-day
No cloud-assailing eagle daunts us more ;
The Grecian flight alone can bring dismay.
    But true Religion bids us soar

Higher than Hæmus and the Hippocrene.
Trumpet and harp her inspiration learn,
And where she builds, O Sophocles, the scene,

    Triumphs a loftier Cothurn.

And what is Pindar unto Bethlehem's son?
The warrior shepherd-boy to Dagon's shame?
The ruddy minstrel of the Holy One,

    Who knew to sing the Eternal Name?

Hear us, O Shades! We dare a heavenward flight,
And daring is our victory's pledge and claim.
With reed in steadfast hand we mete aright

    The scope and fashion of our aim.

Thou who first comest, wert thou not in fight
The blood-stained conqueror, yet the poet's friend?
Yes, thou art CHARLES.[2] Vanish, O Shade, in night,

    Who would'st with blood our faith amend!

---

[2] That is, CHARLEMAGNE, called by the Germans Charles
the Great, without incorporating the words. He offered the
conquered Saxons Christianity or death.

Mount, BARBAROSSA, to a prouder height!
Thine is the elder age of noble song.
For CHARLES in vain before the eye bade trace
    The bardic war-strains, silent long.[3]

It lies forgotten in the convent-crypt,
And low complains in darkness underground,
A bright illumin'd and fair-letter'd script,
    Pledge of his art who first to sound

Gave form in Fatherland, and from decay
Rescued old German deeds before they sank.
'Mid ruins first, and then a ruin, lay
    The proud invention of the Frank.

It calls and shakes (but thou hear'st not, O friar!)
The golden studs.   It smites with angry bound
The 'scutcheon'd cover.   Him who hears, my lyre
    Tells grateful to the echoes round.

---

[3] Charlemagne procured the Songs of the Bards to be committed to writing, which had hitherto been handed down by oral tradition. The historian Paris had seen some of these copies. Frederic Barbarossa became Emperor of Germany in 1152.

Thou sang'st thyself, O HENRY : " Mine, in troth,
Are crown and land. The crown I'd rather miss,
I'd rather want (though ye are welcome both)
    Pageant and power than part with THIS !"

If now thou livedst, noblest of thy land,
And Cæsar, would'st thou—while the Germans burned
To strive with Hæmus' bards, and those that stand
    By Tarquin's Fane—sleep unconcerned ?

Thou sangest, HENRY : " Me they serve who bring
Ploughshare or lance. But I would rather lose
The crown, than gems that longer grace a king
    Than crowns, fair honours and the Muse !"

THE FUTURE.

THE heavenly ear can list the moving spheres,
And where Seleno and Pleione roll
 In thunder, and rejoicing hears
 The sounds that swell beneath the-pole,

When swift the planet in its orbit flees,
And when the worlds, in golden lustre lost,
 Circle each other : then the seas
 Answer the whirlwind, tempest toss'd—

The sea of Hesper—seas of earth and moon
More gently.   But how high the billows roar
 In far Boötes, and are thrown
 In thunder on the rocky shore !

Clear waves the Altar there on high, and here
The golden Queen, whose right hand bears the palm :
 Clear sails the Swan, and clear
 The Rose, so dewy calm.

The psalmody resounds. Before the King,
Spirits made perfect in their high abode,
 Triumph and adoration sing,
 And thank—for they can thank—their God.

What yearning stirs within me ! sense obscure
Of joys, that, breathing solace inexpress'd,
 Shall in the dust the dust assure
 Inward and everlasting rest !

Soft whispers, wafted from the songs divine
Of sons of glory, visit oft below
 Earth's laden pilgrims, and benign
 Dry up the tears that silent flow.

Ye radiant worlds, through all your empire strays
One being weak as man ? E'en us who weep,
 Death, our deliverer, dismays !
 Though soft he come in cloudy sleep

He stands before us dreadful !   The abyss
Is all we see beneath us ; though from night
    He bear us safe to perfect bliss
    And to the land of clearer light;

And up the stony path of Patience mount
To Paradise and bless'd societies —
    Mount from this life, which near its fount
    Lingers 'mid rocks, or hastening flees

To where the spring-flowers blossom but to fade,
Glittering with dew and od'rous in the vale—
    A life that, hastening or delay'd,
    Is ended as an idle tale.

SIONA.

SOUND ! harp of the palm-grove,
Playmate of songs that David sang !
The strains of Zion soar above
The fount that from the impinging hoof upsprang.[1]

O grove, from higher cloud
Thou lookest on the laurel-wood below.
Thy shadows are the laurel's shroud,
Thrown from the golden clouds that round thee glow.

---

[1] Hippocrene, fabled to have sprung from the stamping of Pegasus.

SIONA moves where glances
PHIALA'S silver-sounding spray,
    Triumphant through the holy dances,
In faith sublime of Him who lives for aye.

And where she passes call
Soft murmurs from the palmy crest,
    And by the crystal fountain-fall
From hill to hill her triumph is confess'd.

Ardent she looks : her brows
The wreaths of Sharon's rose enfold.
    Like mist, her robe around her flows,
Ting'd with the hues of morn, purple and gold.

O Shulamite, mine eye
Greets thee with glad and loving gaze.
    Sadness, and peace, and rapturous joy,
Thrill through my heart responsive to thy lays.

Hear ye ?   She wakes the lute,
The holy groves with song resound.
    The crystal fountain, listening mute,
Stands still ; the palms in murmurs wave around.

But now the joyous fountain

Leaps headlong.   For SIONA takes

The trumpet, and through all the mountain

Sends the loud blast ; the vale the thunder shakes.

THE IMITATOR.

If other strain affright thee than the lay
   Of Greece, O Teuton, not to thee belong
Hermann, and Luther, Leibnitz, and all they
   Who listen in the grove to Braga's song.

Thou art no German bard of native fire,
   Who bearest slavishly an alien yoke.
No field of Marathon did thee inspire,
   Thou had'st no sleepless nights, when Genius woke.

TUISCO.

WHEN the rays of twilight fade, and soft the evening star
Throws a cloudless cool-refreshing glimmer from afar,
Deep descending on the grove, in which the bards are crown'd,
And wherein melodiously the MIMER-springs resound,

Then the spirit of TUISCO, like the silver dew
Of the scatter'd waterfall, descends and comes to you,
Ye bards, and to the fountain. There the oak anon
Murmurs to him gently, like the Venusinian swan,

When, transform'd, he thither flew. TUISCO hears, and roves
Listening to the wavy rustle of the greeting groves.
But his children now surround him, and with louder strain
Welcome him with lute and harp-string to the grove again.

Melodies, as from the Telyn in Walhalla, throng

From the changing, bolder echoes of Teutonian song ;

Now upsoaring, like the eagle to the summer clouds,

Now descending to the oak-top which the fountain shrouds,

SKATING.

Sunk in the tomb of endless night
    Lies many a great inventor's name :
Our torch we kindle at their light ;
    But where is their reward of fame ?

How name ye him, who ocean cross'd
    First with tall mast and swelling sheet?
I would not e'en his name were lost
    Who added wings to flying feet.

For should he not immortal live,
    Whose art can health and joy enhance,
Such as no mettled steed can give,
    Such, e'en, as pants not in the dance ?

Undying still be thy renown !
  The ice-dance, with the gliding steel,
I trace, inventive ; flying down
  The course, then turn with finer heel.

Thou knowest each inspiring tone
  Of Music.   Lend it to the dance !
Her horn resound to wood and moon,
  When rapidly she bids advance !

O youth, whose skill the ice-cothurn
  Drives glowing now, and now restrains,
On city hearths let fagots burn,
  But come with me to crystal plains !

The scene is fill'd with vapoury light,
  As when the winter morning's prime
Looks on the lake.   Above it Night
  Scatters, like stars, the glittering rime.

How still and white is all around !
  How rings the track with new-sparr'd frost !
Far off the metal's cymbal-sound
  Betrays thee, for a moment lost.

The wallet bears enough, I ween,

    Of cates and gladsome wine in store?

The winter air makes hunger keen,

    And the foot's flying pinions more.

Turn to the left! I will incline

    My course, half circling, to the right.

Lean forward! take thy stroke from mine!

    So—now shoot by me, like the light!

In undulation serpentine

    Along the shore we downward wend.

Poise not thy attitudes too fine!

    Such turns I love not, nor commend.

Why to the Isle dost list aloof?

    Unpractised skaters clamour there.

The ice not yet will load and hoof

    Above, nor nets beneath it, bear.

Ah! nought upon thine ear is lost.

    What wailing doth the death-crash make!

How different sounds it, when the frost

    Runs, splitting, miles along the lake!

Turn back ! nor let the glacial gleam
　　Entice thee onward far from shore !
For there perchance deep waters stream,
　　And there the bubbling fountains pour.

By waves unheard above the reef,
　　By hidden springs, Death watches nigh.
Though thou glide lightly as the leaf,
　　There would'st thou sink, young man, and die !

THE YOUTH.

In silvery brook beneath the thorn
   May saw his locks wave light in air ;
His wreath was rosy as the morn,
   He smiled to see himself so fair.

The tempest from the hills came down.
   Oak, ash, and pine-tree felt the shock.
The maple from the mountain's crown
   Rush'd headlong with the shiver'd rock.

Peaceful he slumber'd by the brook,
   Let the storm thunder near and far.
He slept, while blossoms o'er him shook,
   And wak'd up with the evening star.

Thou knowest nought of Misery.

Fair as the Graces smile thy days.

Up! gird on Wisdom's panoply!

For soon, fond youth, the bloom decays.

EARLY GRAVES.

WELCOME, O silver Moon,
　　Fair, still companion of the night !
Friend of the pensive, flee not soon !
　　Thou stayest — and the clouds pass light.

Young waking May alone
　　Is fair as summer night so still,
When from his locks the dews drop down,
　　And, rosy, he ascends the hill.

Ye noble souls and true,
　　Whose graves with sacred moss are strawn,
Blest were I, might I see with you,
　　The glimmering night, the rosy dawn !

BATTLE-SONG.

How rung the trampling warrior-throng
Down to the vale from mountain height,
Where by the woodstream call'd the battle-song
To furious onset and avenging fight!

To victory and daring deeds,
To the deliverer's proud renown!
There they await us where the torrent speeds
And, thunder-arm'd, the crests of battle crown.

Oh, each is but a tyrant's slave!
Before the threatening faulchion free,
Before the approach and voices of the brave,
Who give themselves to Death, they turn and flee!

THE OUTER COURT AND THE TEMPLE.

Who tires to gaze upon the starry sky
When Hesper sinks in ocean, and on high
The Fish and Scorpion glitter, and resplendent shine
The Lion, and the Wheat-ears, and the Dresser of the Vine?

With dread, and awe, and rapture at the sight
His heart is filled who yearns for true delight.
No phantoms mock him. In the outer court divine
I stand, till, winged by death, my spirit seeks the inner shrine.

Thou, Midnight, hear my song! thou Star of Morn,
Find me, 'mid praise and thanks, to tears o'erborne!
Herald of Day, if thou the Evening Star become,
Find me adoring God, whose marvellous mercy holds me dumb!

THE GREAT HALLELUJAH.

GLORY to God supreme! the first, the Father
Of all creation! whom our stammering Psalms
    Would praise; though He is wonderful
    Beyond the aim of speech and thought!

A flame from off the altar by the throne
Hath stream'd into our souls.   And we rejoice
    With heavenly joy both that we are,
    And that Him, wondering, we admire!

Glory to Him from dwellers 'mid the tombs!
Though on the lowest step of His high throne
    The archangel's diadem, cast down,
    Rings with the rapture of his song.

Glory, and thanks, and praise, to the Supreme!
The First, whose years begun not, nor shall end;
    Who gave to dwellers in the dust
    Beginning, but no end of days.

Glory to Him, the Wonderful, who sow'd
The ocean of Infinity with worlds!
    And fill'd them with undying hosts,
    To love Him, and in Him be blest.

All glory, glory, glory be to Thee!
O'er all supreme, before all creatures first!
    The Father of the Universe,
    Unspeakable and unconceiv'd!

BRAGA.

BY WANDOR, WITTEKIND'S BARD.

Dost waste in woodlands with the herd thy time,
And musing slumberest? nor arouseth thee,
O Tenderling, December's silver rime,
　　Nor star-lights on the crystal sea?

I mock to see thee crouch'd in the wolf's hide
Before the fire, yet bloody from the wound,
Where the keen arrow pierced the conqueror's side,
　　When he sank helpless to the ground.

Up, then, awake! December never cross'd
The woodlands with so bright, so soft a ray;
Nor hoar-white blossoms after nightly frost
　　Flower'd so fair at dawn of day.

Already with the glow of health elate
Descending swift the frozen shore along,
The crystal I have whiten'd with my skate
    In mazes, as to Braga's song.

Beneath the volant foot and metal keen,
Light borne along the ice, fleet echoes rise.
Over the mosses by the margin green
    My flying shadow with me flies.

But now the cloudless moon ascends the sky.
Her inspiration all my soul pervades
As drunk at Mimer's fountain! I descry,
    Far off beneath the bardic shades,

Braga, whose shoulder with no quiver rings,
But 'neath his foot, like silver, sounds the steel.
From night into the moonbeam forth he springs,
    And skims the crystal with light heel.

Sing how the oak-leaves bound his brow sublime.
Sing, Bardic song, how, as with pearly dew,
The wreath of Glasor glitter'd with the rime :
    His golden locks were rimy too.

Fiery he woke the strings, and taught the rock
The Telyn's minstrelsy.   The brave his lays
Rewarded, and the wise : the strophe's stroke
    Rung joyous forth Walhalla's praise.

" Ha ! how my lance is bloody, and calls down
The eagle from the cloud."   Along the dance,
Thus singing, like the storm he hastened on,
    Or slacken'd now to slow advance.

" Strike your strong pinions, eagles, for the prey !
Come ! drink warm blood !"   Through the dim-glittering air
He scour'd along the course.   The God of day,
    Apollo, never sped so fair.

Then lighter turns, disportive, him beseem'd,
And lighter Telyn-tones.   " Hear, grove, my strain !
Not by the Hebrus, as the Grecian deem'd,
    Upon the crystal water-plain,

These wings of steel that can the storm o'ertake,
Did Thracian Orpheus find, nor down the flood
Sped to Eurydice ; but I, who wake
    To heroes in the sacred wood

My songs, and Bard and Scald with fire inform.
I — sound it, Telyn, to the Hebrus ! — I
Invented these, the wingèd shaft and storm,
    In race victorious to outvie.

The art I taught to Siphia's beauteous son,[1]
Around whose foot and arrow lightnings played.
I taught it Tialf, whom in contest none
    Outstripped, as erst the Sorcerer's shade.

I taught the bravest of the northern kings ;
Yet him did Russia's proud Eliza shun.
Would Nossa,[2] whom the harp immortal sings,
    Would she have fled him, foolish one ?"

He sped. His frosty garland crisp'd aloud,
Back flew his golden hair. The steelly clang
Mellow'd in distance ; till in misty cloud
    His form was lost where heights o'erhang.

---

[1] Siphia's son—Uller.
Tialf — Thor's attendant, who held a race with an illusive
Giant, raised by sorcery. See Prose Edda.
[2] The goddess of grace and beauty.

THE SUMMER NIGHT.

When o'er the woods that sleep below
The moonbeam pours her gentle light,
And odours of the lindens flow
　　On the cool airs of night,

Thoughts overshade me of the tomb,
Where my beloved rest.　I see
In the deep forest nought but gloom,
　　No blossom breathes to me.

Such nights, ye dead, with you I pass'd !
How cool and od'rous stream'd the air !
The moonbeam then, so gently cast,
　　Made Nature's self more fair !

THE GRAVES OF ROTHSCHILD.

(ON THE DEATH OF FREDERIC V. OF DENMARK.)

AH! here they have interr'd thee, son with sire,
  Thee whom we loved, for whom yet flows the tear,
Pledge of the unforgetting heart's desire,
  Saddening the cheek with recollections dear.

Should not a people pour above his tomb
  True tears, who wak'd no widow's lorn lament?
And long bewail a father-king, from whom
  The orphan came with tears of deep content?

I turn away, I cannot seek the pile,
  Where the dead sleeps beside the dead who slept,
Beside Luisa, who bade sorrow smile
  Till o'er herself unsolac'd sorrow wept,

Ye long-departed dust,—once kings ! how soon
    For you the Great Supreme your grandchild claims !
Awed with death-thoughts I rove from stone to stone,
    And read the letters there that seem like flames !

Not such as tell but of the outward deed,
    Nor know the aim, which ne'er the soul betray'd.
Dread gleams the holy sentence : " There they plead
    Where shine the radiant crowns that never fade."

Still sunk in gloomier thoughts I shun the tomb
    Where from the throne our Frederic sank to earth.
For my heart bleeds for him.   Oh, night of gloom,
    When God sow'd here the seed of heavenly birth !

Why do I shrink and yet avoid the grave,
    Where he shall one day wake with kindred clay ?
Is it not God, who to the furrow gave
    The seed that blooms in everlasting day ?

And shall his heart be weak still, who hath lost
    So many friends belov'd,—more blest than he ?
Whose thoughts can summon a celestial host,
    When he looks o'er this brief mortality ?

And sees by graves the dwellings where men dream,
  Till death awakes them to true life at last?
Be strong, my heart, nor let it dreadful seem
  To see that kingly form when life is pass'd!

Strew flowers around! the spring is come again;
  Come without him! let blossoms crown his tomb
Denmark's fair custom, that in hope is fain
  Yearly to strew the peasant's grave with bloom,

Be brightly kept: and o'er the kingly urn
  Spread garlands for the Resurrection meet!
Mild, cheering image of that spring's return!
  And shall our eyes with tears those garlands greet?

O Fred'ric, Fred'ric, all beside is fled
  But a cold corpse that hastens to decay.
And thou, dumb tomb, dost shadow o'er the dead
  With tardy wings of darkness and dismay.

I hear ye waver, spirits of the shade!
  Who are ye? "We were fathers once, in life;
And bless the spot where Frederic is laid!
  We come not from the fields of mortal strife."

P

The sound is lost in distance, and I hear
   That passing host no more.   Sorrow's dark cloud
Alone hangs o'er me.   Whom I held so dear
   Sleeps there beneath me, mantled in death's shroud !

E'en as a native of the land, home-born,
   Fred'ric I loved : and with him sleeps my heart.
Thee, best of kings, the Muse's son shall mourn,
   And Wisdom's, and the favourite of Art.

Thee, best of kings, young, old, the sick, the poor,
   Weep as a father — all thy people weep !
From Heckla's pyre is heard to Weser's shore
   The wail of all thy people, loud and deep !

If deathless fame reward thee, 'tis begun.
   But can thy recompense be earthly fame ?
O son of Frederic, O Luisa's son,
   Fulfil the hope and promise of thy name.

Fair, noble youth, bedeck'd with every grace,
   With Virtue most, thy Father's pathway keep !
To thee no fane is holier than this place,
   Where in their honour'd graves thy fathers sleep.

They tell that all is vanity below :

That Virtue's deeds survive that day alone,

Which shall destroy all earthly crowns, and show

The crowns of life before the Judge's throne !

SKULDA.[1]

In th' inmost grove I learnt,
   What loud poetic lays
Sink into dark oblivion's vale,
   Or greet upon the hills the morning rays.

I saw — and tremble still —
   The NORNA's judging eyes :
I heard, and hear, her lofty wings
   Sonorous to the oak-wood's summit rise.

---

[1] SKULDA, the Norn, or Destiny of the Future, as WERANDI and WURDI were of the Present and Past.

Cooled by the wavy spring
 Sat BRAGA, leaning light
Upon his lyre. And spirits now
 WERANDI brought, whom in the moonlit night

Hither she lur'd from songs,
 And sheath'd in bodies meet
Each for its spirit ; every trait
 Rendering in form and counterpart complete.

Ten were they, that drew near.
 One only seem'd to scan
Far fame ; and blush'd with conscious worth,
 Full of the charm of youth and strength of man.

With rev'rence he advanced,
 When he the Norna saw,
Who leads to the far hills of dawn,
 Or down to night which endless clouds o'erdraw.

Reflective SKULDA spread
 Her broad o'ershading wings,
Though still her oaken wand sank down,
 Whose signal-stroke to fools no warning brings.

The Nine tread proud the grove :
 With ravish'd ear they hail
The chattering of the noisy throng,
 And of uncertain judges in the vale.

The smile in SKULDA'S eyes
 Them scared not.　They were laid,
Sweetly deceived, on wreaths asleep,
 Which they saw bloom in dreams, but saw not fade.

Ah ! NORNA rose in flight,
 And motion'd with her wand
Valewards.　They glided without noise,
 By short or longer way, into that vale profound.

But with that one she turn'd
 Towards the hills of day.
Her wings resounded, like the lute,
 And her staff pointed the immortal way.

SELMA AND SELMAR.

" Oh ! weep not ! whom I loved so dear,
That Fate has torn me from thee here !
When Hesper smiles upon thee clear,
  I come again,—all blest."

Thou climb'st the hills in sable night,
Wavest o'er lakes in dimmer light :
Shar'd I with thee death's dread affright,
  Should I yet weep — all blest ?

WE AND THEY.

WHAT ails thee for thy Fatherland ?
If at its name unmoved thou stand
        I scorn thee and disdain.

True, they are rich and proud beside :
We are not rich, we have no pride,
        That is our better gain.

Honest we are ; which scarce they seem ;
Haughty they stand, and haughtier dream.
        We mock no alien's birth.

Genius is theirs of lofty powers ;
Such lofty genius too is ours.
        That gives us equal worth.

The subtlest science of the wise
They to the marrow scrutinise.
  We too—and long have done.

Whom have they, that, with soaring flight,
Like HANDEL can the soul delight?
  There we at least have won.

Whom among them can skilful throw
O'er pencill'd forms the spirit's glow?
  E'en KNELLER we supplied.

When does their minstrel reach the heart?
He weeps in tropes. O land of Art,
  Hellas, the cause decide!

They smite in the sulphureous war,
Where, ship to ship, the thunders roar:
  We too could smite as they.

They hasten to the tented strand,
To battles that we understand;
  From us they flee away.

Oh ! if we saw them in that field,
Where well we understand to wield
　　The keen-edg'd battle-tool,

HERMANNS themselves our chiefs would boast,
CHERUSCANS would be all our host,
　　CHERUSCANS bold and cool.

What ails thee for thy Fatherland?
If at its name unmov'd thou stand,
　　I scorn thee, craven fool !

OUR PRINCES.

FROM the Palm mountain, from Siona's hill,
We come, the minstrels of the Psaltery,
    If haply Christian hearts we fill
    With fire that heavenward mounts on high.

Here in the grove, with oak-leaves shadow'd o'er,
To thee, O Telyn, fairer strains belong,
    When Moral Beauty sounds before
    The beauty of artistic song.

I rove with rapture where the palms expand ;
And here, with joy, 'mid oak-shades dread and dim
    Of us, O bards, our Fatherland
    Demands a patriotic hymn.

Race of Tuisco, wear the joyous crown,
The sacred wreath that Braga loves to bring;
    He brings it from the mountain down,
    All dripping bright from Mimer's spring.

The tones, ye bards, of exultation swell
From Braga's harp; ye are his proud delight!
    With him ye drank at Mimer's well
    High wisdom and poetic might.

Why do ye pause? Ye triumph'd over time
When felt the Princes of our Fatherland
    No pride to cherish song sublime.
    And ye—whoever might withstand—

Soar'd a bold flight alone with eagle eye.
So shall your fame unnumber'd ages fill,
    When names of princes fade and die,
    Like Echo, when the voice is still.

Ah! never from Tuisco's grove arise
Soft tones to grace a Parian monument,
    Which none regards; which quickly lies
    With mouldering bones in ruin blent

How joyously the grove resounds!   I see
The flying dance, the triumph BRAGA leads.
    They thunder " Immortality,"
    The echoes fill the woods and meads.

Old Pyramids have sunk, and whirlwinds sweep
The ruins still.   Encomiums that did crave
    Nought but the smile of princes, sleep
    In gilded halls as in the grave.

Lie low, ye Pyramids! ye flatterers' strains
Sleep in your golden crypt, and wake no more!
    Us deathless Genius sustains,
    And boldness bids us freely soar

In scorn of recompense.   Your time to aid
Is pass'd, ye princes!   Build your marble tomb,
    To rest forgotten in the shade!
    For in the grave your praise is dumb.

BATTLE-SONG.

By our own arm is nothing wrought,
If He, the Mighty, help us not,
   Who orders all.

In vain we thirst for daring deeds,
If He give not the victor's meeds,
   Who orders all.

In vain our blood is on the blade
For Fatherland, unless He aid,
   Who orders all.

For Fatherland flow blood and death!
In Him we put our steadfast faith
   Whose will doth all dispose.

Up ! to where breathes the battle's breath !
For we have smil'd to look on death,
    And smile on you, our foes !

To beat of drums as we advance,
How glorious is the battle-dance,
    That onward sweeps to you !

There sound the trumpets ! Hew the way
Where our red steel hath carv'd to-day
    An open passage through.

The onset which the trumpet sounds,
How loud and joyous it resounds !
    Haste !· haste with wingèd speed !

There where our columns forward flow,
There wave the standards to and fro,
    There triumph man and steed !

See ye the crest that wavers white ?
See ye the sword above the fight ?
    The marshal's sword and crest ?

He orders where the battle bleeds,
And where decisive action needs
    Offers a dauntless breast.

Through him and us is nothing wrought,
If He, the Mighty, help us not,
    Whose will doth all dispose.

Away! where breathes the sulphury breath!
Away! for we have smiled on death,
    And smile on you, our foes!

THE QUIRES.

O GOLDEN dream, still but a dream to me,
Bright, radiant image, beauteous as the morn,
    Come yet on wings of ecstasy
        Before my vision borne !

Wear they their crowns in vain? nor blissful turn
That dream to brightness of celestial grace?
    O'er them must close their marble urn,
        When that bright change takes place?

Son of the Highest, to thy glory free
The loftiest lyre resounds with loftiest song.
    Thy work was perfect : unto thee
        Worship and praise belong.

Q

Thee — if the grave but let me — I would sing!
Though not to loftiest lyre resound my lays:
    Yet would I draw from joy's deep spring,
      Inspired, thy perfect praise.

Great is thy work, and great is my desire!
He knows not rapture's overpow'ring spell,
    Who never felt the sacred fire
      Flame bright at Music's swell:

Nor to the pealing of the holy psalm
Hath gently trembled, when the temple's quires
    Were heard, and — if this sea were calm —
      ·The sound of heavenly lyres!

Blest dream, entrance me long! I hear the burst
Of Christian song. What multitudes are one!
    So Cephas saw five thousand erst
      Bow to the anointed Son.

Hark! how they praise the Child of Heavenly Birth,
One in simplicity of heart and tongue!
    And glory greater than of earth
      Ascends to heaven in song.

Rapture transports them, and a moisten'd eye
Gleams through the strain. The crown of glory stands
    Radiant before them : they descry
        The palms in saintly hands.

Now the psalm opens from the choral band,
And music, inartistic, from full hearts
    Flows streaming forth : the masters stand
        Leading their several parts.

It sinks into the living soul with might,
Contemning all that wakens not the tear,
    Nor fills the breast with rapt delight,
        Nor heavenly thoughts severe.

For thoughts severe with festive notes have place.
And Prophecy, in seed-time and in bloom,
    Alternate fills the quire. And Grace,
        By turns, they sing, and Doom.

By Jesu's love, by Zion's holy throng
Inflamed, they bid their thankfulness arise.
    A single voice begins the song,
        A single harp replies.

But soon a mightier music fills the quire,
The choral strain ascends on loftier wing;
  The people glow with heavenly fire
   And tremble while they sing.

Their joy they scarce contain.   The trumpet loud
Wakes thunder, and again the thunder wakes.
  The chorus of the mingled crowd
   Sounds, till the temple shakes.

No more! no more!   The multitude in praise
Fall on their faces tow'rd the inner fane.
  Pure from the chalice, haste, and raise
   The glad triumphant strain!

Fast by the temple lay my weary bones!
That o'er my dust may sound the people's psalm.
  My tomb shall vibrate to the tones,
   The flower above breathe balm.

When, like the light that breaks on them that die,
The songs that hail the resurrection wave,
  There where I hear them shall reply
   A harp-note from the grave.

THE BARDS.

Ye Bards, the shroud of night
        The Telyn does invest,
Which often Braga heard with mute delight,
When high Invention, slumbering in the West,

        Fair form and spirit bare,
        Beauteous as boys in battle-dance;
Till ravish'd, when she saw what forms they were,
Her sight before her swam in wilder'd glance.

        Forward a Genius spings
        Through the oak-grove to roam.
Harmonious is his tread : his footfall rings
Light as the brook, or loud as torrent's foam.

Ye Bards, where sank in night
The Telyn of our chiefs ?
Ah ! when I think what ruin hides from sight,
Mine eye grows dim with unavailing griefs !

TEONE.[1]

THE song lay silent on the page — in dread
Before the raving Rhapsodist, who read
    With noisy emphasis unknown
    To gentle voice and mellow tone.

There where he scream'd was Homer.   His conceit
Made him a judge, but hid the witless cheat.
    The flow of song was dash'd to froth,
    The Poet's genius fled in wrath.

---

[1] The word is formed from the name of a rhetorician of
Alexandria, who lived in the reign of Marcus Aurelius, and in
its feminine usage is made to personify his art.

E'en thou, O Songstress, learn TEONE's art,
That moulds like wax the language to the part.
 In turn and cadence meet to play
 With the true spirit of the lay.

Hear her, to ranting vehemence severe,
Avenge the song, and form it to the ear.
 Are not these turns of finer tone,
 Music melodious as thine own ?

A melody that is the heart's confession
Of inmost feeling ? and a clear expression,
 Flute-like, or like thy notes that rise
 Above the flute-notes to the skies ?

Why dost thou tremble ? Wherefore from thine eye
Falls fast the tear ? What makes thy bosom sigh ?
 Is't not TEONE's tender tone ?
 Or does the poet move alone ?

Hers is his minstrelsy ! The subtlest turn
Of art and song TEONE can discern.
 Her follow, as with grace sublime
 She leads the lofty dance of rhyme.

Plant for her flowers by MIMER's vocal spring,
Nossa ! that if she grace the lays I sing
    With tones that tell the feeling there,
    My wreath may twine TEONE's hair.

STINTENBURG.

O ISLE, where Solitude is sweet,
  Beloved of Echo, and the lake
That spreads out now its glassy sheet,
Now sweeps in rushing stream round hill and brake,

Itself with many a bank beset,
  Where lampreys sport in sedgy nook,
And shun the wily fisher's net,
And pity the poor worm upon the hook ;

But a few passing hours I stray'd
  In sound of thy melodious reeds ;
But from my memory ne'er shall fade
Thine image, fair as forms that Fancy leads

To triumph o'er forgetfulness.
  The prince's garden is o'ergrown
With bush and brake ; but not the less
High art endures above the waste alone.

Beside thee frowns the Saxon's weald.

   Short was his speech and swift his sword.

   Round thee ne'er gleam'd the Roman shield,

Nor eagle, sent by Rome's imperial lord.

   Serenely wander'd through thy vale

     That goddess dear, the gentle HLYN ;

   And BRAGA's harp upon the gale

Flung its glad lay, unmix'd with battle's din.

   Save that, adown the prouder flood

     Where roll'd the forest to the sea,

   There BRAGA's harp was stain'd with blood,

And at his threatening song the lances flee.

   But to her bath when HERTHA drew,[1]

     BRAGA return'd and linger'd here :

   Spring did her melodies renew ;

In rhythmic dance the god let fall the spear.

---

[1] The image of Hertha (mother Earth) was drawn about in procession at springtime, and finally bathed in a secret lake, by which she was refreshed ; in symbolic representation (it should seem) of the renovation of Nature.

His harp-notes still are heard ; and oft
    I catch the old Teutonic tone,
When walks the unclouded moon, and soft
Swells round his hero's grave the Telyn's moan.

Listening that lay, I too might sing,
    O Isle, the Planter of thy land,
And follow him on raptured wing
Through tracks of deathless fame, with wreath in hand.

But desecrated was the art
    That woke the adulator's lay,
And, seldom just to true desert,
Rung in his ear, who, featless, pass'd away.

Harp of the sacred Bardic throng,
    Disown the honour-waster's strain,
Who to false glitter gave his song,
Which deeds of worthlessness forbade in vain !

O reckless prodigal ! they trust
    No more in minstrels honour'd long—
Perish, e'en as the crumbling dust
Of yonder ruin, thy perverted song !

Coldly incredulous they hear
   The wingèd silver tones that ring
   E'en to the oak-tops, loud and clear,
To tell his merit whom ye idly sing.

   Through thee, profane! my heart no more
     Feels inspiration true and strong.
   Perish—as crumbles to the shore
You ruin,—perish thy perverted song!

OUR NATIVE TONGUE,

OR TEUTONA.[1]

On the height where MIMER's fountain o'er the vale below
Flings into a cloud of silver its melodious flow,
I beheld the goddess : bear me witness, sacred wood,
Down she came to meet the mortal and before me stood.

Lofty was her stature : and around her saw I throng
Spirits she had charm'd from the departed forms of song,
Still delusive by their likeness.   They whom WURDI's dirk[2]
Blameless smote, did follow distant and in twilight lurk.

---

[1] I have given two titles, because in the original the verses which
are entitled " Teutona" are but a slight variation of those which are
here translated.   Only three or four stanzas are varied.

[2] Wurdi's dagger represents the destructive power of the Past.

They whom SKULDA's wand more mighty from oblivious night
Rescued, round the goddess flutter'd, triumphing in light.
And the gleam was bright about them, and they proudly spoke ;
And their temples they had garlanded with leaves of oak.

To give utterance to Thought with feeling and with power,
And with turns of boldness stamp the passion of the hour,
That to thee, O goddess of TUISCO's native tongue,
Is a sport, as to the heroes were the deeds they sung.

Inspiration ! lo, she rises ! and her glances throw
Fiery flashes round her, and her soul is in the glow !
Stream thee forth ! for the insensate thou dost spare in vain.
Void of feeling he can never to thy thought attain.

Now she waves about the fount-fall ! mighty is the tone,
when the winds along the outskirts of the forest moan.
Now above, around, the rocks the gathering tempests pour.
Thrillingly the traveller listens to the forest's roar.

Now she waves about the fountain ? gentle is the sound
the sighing of the zephyrs in the woods profound.
Now above, around, the rocks the gathering tempests hie ;
Thrillingly the traveller listens to the forest's sigh.

O thou freeborn, thee the stranger never did profane.
Still unconquer'd thou hast known alone the victor's bane.
Never hast thou felt the fetter, to thy fear and hurt :
The eagles have departed ; thou remainest what thou wert.

Still beside the Rhodanus, before the victor proud,
Loud is heard the clank of chains ; beside the Iber, loud.
E'en to thee, Britannia, resounds along thy coast
Lordly triumph of the Angle and the Saxon host.

So prevail'd not by the Rhine the race of Romulus,
Just reward and full requital were pronounced by us,—
Vengeance of the German sword and of the German tongue !
The chains were roll'd in Varus' blood to expiate the wrong.

Thee too, then, our Speech, they rescued, when in Weser's wood
There the victor's chains for ever sank beneath the flood —
Silent sank in blood of legions slaughter'd in the fight,
Evermore to lie forgotten in the shroud of night.

Ah ! the spirits of the Bardic songs, that did resound
To that host of patriots battling for their native ground,
Follow with the wounded to untimely sepulture,
Wounded, WURDI, by thy dagger, wounded beyond cure !

Wilt thou slay therewith the spirit that laments the slain ?
Phantoms, Spirits, Genii, of song inspire my strain.
Teach me, lead me, by the arduous and bolder way,
Through the forest to the height where sounds the deathless lay.

Thee, O Ossian ! thee, Forgetfulness doth darkly shroud,
But they now upraise thee, and thou lookest o'er the crowd.
To the Greek thou dost compare thee, and demandest bold,
If he pour'd, like thee, the flame into his song of old.

Full of thought APOLLO heard him with reflective mien,
.Heard but made no answer.   On his harp did BRAGA lean,
.Right before APOLLO standing by Walhalla's fane,
-And he smiled, and he was silent ; but he look'd not with disdain.

TIALF'S ART.

BY WITTEKIND'S[1] BARDS,

BLIID, HAINING, AND WANDOR.

BLIID.

How rings the ice ! Stay thy impetuous feet !
　The night-breath glimmers o'er the frozen seas !
Still on thou speedest !　From a course too fleet
　Affrighted NOSSA flees.

---

[1] WITTEKIND, an able chief of the Saxons who defended them against the invasions of Charlemagne.　NOSSA is the goddess of grace.

HAINING.

She follows after.   I in rhythmic dance

O'ertake the shaft fresh-wingèd from the bow.

How the smooth plain resounds to my advance !

Is Nossa's foot too slow ?

BLIID.

Provoke her not, o'ertaker of the reed !

Scorn'd she returns no more.   I see it now,

Her anger is begun : hold in thy speed !

The cloud is on her brow.

HAINING.

Dost see them by the rock come down the lake

In the clear air of bright December morn ?

How they wave onward !   Dearly will I take

Revenge of Hlyda's scorn.

BLIID.

Who comes ? who is it ?   How they shed a ray

Of brightness on December's morn so fair !

Ha ! thou defamer of the goddess, say,

Who wave through the white air ?

Like huntsman's echo from the valley's sides
    The crystal rings melodious to the steel :
And many swing about the chair that glides
        As on self-moving keel.

And who is she, with ermeline beclad,
    Who back-reclining on her chair so light
Lists to the youth behind her, who would add
        Wings to the steel-borne flight ?

HAINING.

'Twas for the maiden's sake I did defame
    Fair NOSSA ; nor to pardon is she loth.
The youth and maiden own their mutual flame,
        To-day they seal their troth.

O thou, beclad in ermeline, and thou,
    Whose flying hair is bright with silver rime,
Our bardic dance shall celebrate with you
        The festival sublime.

WANDOR.

Be welcome, brothers ! Well ye ply your feet
　Along the shore with whistling rushes crown'd.
Yet one condition :— Make we no retreat
　　Until the moon goes down !

Far is it to the dance that in the hall
　With the descending moon begins to reel.
Ye must hold strong.　She who observes us all
　　Loves well the flying steel.

Lo ! there the skater with the sparkling bowl,
　Which the vine-dresser of the Rhine did store
With grape-juice to the brim !　It trembles full :
　　Let not a drop run o'er !

So round about ! and let the horn-notes ring
　To ancient measures of the bridal strain.
And then let Braga's flying dances swing
　　Upon the starry plain !

HAINING.

He sang.   The white-robed Hlyda glided by,
 And horns resounded after.   From the sedge
Of either shore her swift companions fly,
  Pois'd light on the steel's edge.

" How glassy is the frost !   Ah ! yonder clang
 Upon the rock, not here ! and let thy might
Fall on the wood, destructive axe ! " we sang,
  And leant us to the right.

" O crystal, ere thou by the sledger's spike,
 Or sharpen'd hoof, or traveller's goad, be cleft,
Numb'd be the hand that did the anvil strike ! "
  We sang, and wended left.

We sang full many a song of skating-time :
 Of the warm west, that all, alas ! destroys,
When fades the blossom of the nightly rime :—
  Of hotspring that decoys

The youth, unseen, to death. He plunged forlorn,
    Tinged with his blood the stream, then sank, and died !
Of brawny goatherd that on steel-wings borne
        Hastes to o'ertake his bride,

Now by the hundred-colour'd portal-pass
    Rear'd on the Gacier, a triumphal bow
To conquering Winter ! now by meadow grass
        Where the lamb feeds below.—

Of flakes that mar the mirror of the ice,
    They fright the traveller on the crystal plain,
As when in verdant vales the hind descries
        The thunder-drops of rain.

We sang the Northman's snow-skate, with the hide
    Of sea-dog clad. He stoops and shoots below
With lightning speed : then up the snow-hill side
        Mounts toilsomely and slow.

The prey drips bloody. from his shoulder hung.
    But the glad dance of Tialf's votaries
He knows not. Them the whirlwind sweeps along,
        The shore behind them flies.

They, fleet as thought, through widening circles sway,
  As waves the sea-snake in mid ocean lost.
Then sang we timid Ida's first essay
    Upon the glassy frost.

Small was her foot, and glittering was the steel.
  The straps with hoar-frost leaflets she inwove,
And flying-fish, red-spotted.   Then we peal
    Our echoes to the grove :

Then to the ruins of the ancient tower ;
  And skim the stream as on the boreal blast,
Or now on the soft west.   But, ah the hour !
    The moon is sinking fast !

We sought the measur'd dance in the light hall ;
  The crackling hearth with the young firs burnt bright.
We feasted proudly, and slept sound withal,
    Making the day our night.

THE HILL AND THE GROVE.

A POET, A MINSTREL, AND A BARD.

POET.

WHY dost thou listen 'neath the wings of night
　To the far-dying echoes of the Bards?
Hear *me!* They heard me who were first in might;
　Through long Olympiads me the Celt regards.

MINSTREL.

　Let me, Shade, the loss deplore!
　　Leave thy golden lyre unstrung.
　For the Bards are heard no more,
　　Who my fatherland have sung.

Let my tears of sadness fall,
 That through weary ages past
The harp is deaf to BRAGA's call,
 To darkness and oblivion cast.

'Mid the wrecks and waste decay
 Of the ancient Celtic tones,
Moans forth now and then a lay,
 As round graves the death-note moans.

POET.

Sound to the wailer, golden lyre, again !
 Why dost thou weep a waste decay ?
Had it deserved the world-life of my strain,
 Would it have pass'd away ?

MINSTREL.

Erst the heroes strove.   Ye called them Gods and Titans then.
When the Ægis rang no more, nor the rocks were piled again,
When with huge Encedalus high ZEUS the thunderer spoke,
Then in clefts of Pelion the Celtic song awoke.

Ha ! thou bear'st thy head aloft
  For thy younger laurel wreath !
Know'st thou not, Oblivion oft
  Treads the deathless underneath ?

The trembling strings thy genius-flight avow ;
  Long to those silver tones I smiled ;
Peace ! I will fashion to me now
  That song of nature wild.

Less circumscribed in thee and thine,
  Than in the bard, was vocal art.
But nature's voice thou whisperest fine,
  While he pours forth his glowing heart.

O forms that wave on rosy wings of morn,
  Or heave with ocean-billows, cloud bedight,
Or through soft dances of the song are borne
  Beneath the moonbeam of the summer night,

If he, who thinks and feels, yet choose you not
  To be companions of his musings lone,
Arise some bard, from wrecks of time forgot,
  Arise, and all your power disown.

Let thy bewitching song, O shade !
　　Its mightiest flight command ;
But call to me from groves decay'd
　　One bard of Fatherland.

Call one Herminion, who woke
　　His echoes in the grove,
Under the thousand-summer'd oak
　　Beneath whose aged shoot I rove.

POET.

I do adjure thee, all-avenging NORN,
　　By the high song that brought the eagles down,
By the spring dances on the bridal morn,
　　Send me one Bard, one true Herminion !

I hear a rustling in the distance deep,
　　And louder, as he comes, sounds Wurdi's spring ;
The billow-breasting swans before him sweep
　　With hasty-smiting wing.

MINSTREL.

Who comes ? who comes ? For warlike now
   The Telyn thunders in his hand ;
The oak-leaves shade his glowing brow ;
   Yes, 'tis a Bard of Fatherland.

BARD.

Why to the first-born of my later sons
   Show'st thou the laurel proudly at the bourne,
O Greek ? Shall he who for the garland runs
    The waving oak-top scorn ?

Dim-veil'd, indeed, and distant ! for he sees
   The raging WURDI's dagger in my breast !
And with the tempest's speed the moment flees
   To sing the mysteries the Bards confess'd.

POET.

   Sound, lyre, the lighter measure,
    That leads with art the circling Graces.
   Leave the voice of ruder Nature,
    Which the Poet's ear debases.

BARD.

Sing, Telyn, Nature full of soul,
  Whom fairer Graces crown.
Art should obey us ; if she dare control,
  She frightens Nature with her haughty frown.

More rare to us was Fancy's form,
  But sketched with bolder art ;
And warm and true, a tumult and a storm,
  And thousand-fold came voices of the heart.

POET.

Let ZEUS, O Bard, still thunder o'er the abyss :
From cloudy night let twang the silver bow
Of SMINTHEUS : PAN shall pipe ; and ARTEMIS,
  With quiver on her shoulder, fright the roe.

BARD.

Is Hellas, then, TUISCO's Fatherland ?
Clad in white mantle on her peaceful sledge
Rests HERTHA ! Through the grove with Zephyrs fann'd
She moves to her lone bath beyond the sedge.

The twins of ALCIS[1] graved upon the rock
　　The law of Friendship, sacred as an oath ;
First, the long choice of the enchanted look,
　　　And then the eternal troth !

WARA with LÖBNA,[2] Nossa's pride, accord
　　As lute and song, as love and womanhood.
Let BRAGA 'gainst the conqueror shake the sword,
　　And WODEN teach you deeds of peace and good !

MINSTREL.

The fountain of the hill resounds to ZEUS,
　　To WODEN does the MIMER-spring belong.
If I awake from gods of ancient use
　　To phantasies of mythic song,

[1] According to Tacitus (*Germ.* 43), the Castor and Pollux of German mythology. They were worshipped as youthful brothers, but without images.

[2] LÖBNA, as described in the Edda, is " a mild and gracious" goddess, who removes obstacles from the course of true love ; and WARA punishes those who break their plighted troth.

To me there is a nobler spell
  In Bards that 'mid the oak-shades rove.
I linger not by Hæmus' well.
  I seek the fountain in the grove.

POET.

  Her who lists the Barbiton,[3]
    Through the laurel-shaded grass
  Leaping down from Helicon,—
    AGANIPPE—canst thou pass?

MINSTREL.

  I see, O Greek, thy lyre depending
    From the laurels where they sigh,
  The golden strings their music blending,
    And I pass it by.

  For BRAGA leans upon the oak,
    To sing the brave of heart and hand,
  The deathless Telyn.   Without stroke
    It sounds spontaneous, " Fatherland."

---

        [3] The Grecian harp.

I hear the sacred name resound,
  And all the thrilling strings invade.
Whose fame does now the echo sound?
  Comes HERMANN yonder through the shade?

BARD.

Ah! the dread dagger! WURDI calls me hence
  To where below, through WODEN's shady weald,
The noble rove, who in their lands' defence
  Sank on the bloody bosses of the shield!

S

HERMANN.

THE BARDS WERDOMAR, KERDING, AND DARMOND.

WERDOMAR

UPON this stone with ancient moss o'erlaid
　　Rest we, O Bards, and be our song begun.
Let none advance to gaze beneath the shade
　　That shrouds in death Teutonia's noblest son.

For there he lies in blood, whose life
　　Was erst the Roman's secret dread,
When they in triumph to the jocund fife
　　His own THUSNELDA [1] led.

---

[1] She was taken prisoner by Germanicus in his first battle
with Hermann, and afterwards figured in his triumph.

Cast not a glance ! for ye would weep
　To see him lying in his gore.
And not to tears the Telyn's string we sweep :
　We sing of those who die no more !

KERDING.

Bright are my locks of youthful hair,
　And first to-day I girded on the sword.
Arm'd for the first time with the lyre and spear,
　Must I too sing the warrior-lord ?

Ask not too much, O sires, of one so young.
　For I must dry up with my locks of gold
These burning tears, before the harp be strung
　To sing the first of MANA's[2] offspring bold.

DARMOND.

　I weep for frantic ire !
　　Nor would my tears assuage !
　Flow, flow adown my cheek of fire,
　　Ye tears of rage !

---

[2] MANA, son of TUISCO, mythological ancestor of the Germans.

They are not dumb, not mute they flow!
   Hear, HELA,[3] hear their curse of might.
No traitor of the land that laid him low
   Die in the fields of fight.

WERDOMAR.

  See ye the torrent dash
    Down through the rock-defile?
  And the torn fir-trees headlong crash
    For HERMANN's funeral pile?

  Soon is he dust, and laid
    In clay-marl of the tomb:
And with the dust the hallow'd blade,
On which he swore the conqueror's doom.

Thou spirit that hast left his form,
Upon thy flight to SIGMAR[4] stay!
And hear thy people's heart how warm
    It beats for thee to-day!

---

[3] HELA reigned over the dreary region whither the shades of the dead were taken who had not died in fight. The latter were admitted into ODIN's hall.

[4] SIGMAR, Hermann's father.

KERDING.

Tell not THUSNELDA, tell her not,
　Here lies in blood her pride, her joy!
A wife, a hapless mother, tell her not
　Here lies the father of her beauteous boy!

Fetters already has she borne
　The triumph of the foe to swell.
Thou hast a Roman heart, if, thus forlorn,
　To her thou canst the tidings tell.

DARMOND.

What sire begat thee, hapless one!
SEGESTES,[5] with revengeful thirst
His sword did redden in his bleeding son!
Him curse not!—HELA has already curs'd!

WERDOMAR.

Name not SEGESTES, ye that sing!
　His name to mute Oblivion doom;
That, where he lies, her heavy wing
　May darken o'er his tomb!

---

[5] SEGESTES, Thusnelda's father, quarrelled with his son-in-law, and conspired with those who slew him.

The string that sounds the name
    Of HERMANN bears disgrace,
If but one note of scorn and shame
    Denounce the traitor base.

For HERMANN, HERMANN to the mountain-call,
    To the deep grove, the favourite of the brave,
The bards in chorus sing.   In chorus all
    Sing the bold chief who did his country save.

Sister of CANNÆ, WINFELD's fight,
    I saw thee with thy bloody-waving hair,
With flame-glance of avenging might,
    Wave through Walhalla 'mid the minstrels there!

The son of DRUSUS[6] fain
    Would hide thy mouldering monument,—
The blanch'd bones of the fallen slain
    Together in the death-vale blent.

---

[6] Germanicus, the son of Drusus, upon arriving at the spot
of Varus's defeat, found the bones of his fellow-citizens and
buried them.

We suffer'd not, but strew'd in dust the mound.

    For these are vouchers of the mighty rout ;

And they shall hear, when flowers are on the ground,

    The war-dance and the victor's shout.

Sisters to CANNÆ would he yet have given,

    With VARUS many a Roman would have laid.

Had not the rival chiefs for envy striven,

    CÆCINA had sought VARUS' shade !

In HERMANN's soul of fire

    Slumber'd a thought of mighty will.

At midnight by THOR's altar to the lyre

    He form'd his vow, impetuous to fulfil.

He thought thereon, when at the high repast

    The warriors danced amid the lances gay ;

And round about the daring dance he cast

    The blood-rings — to the boys a play.

The storm-toss'd mariner his tale resolves :

    " Far in the north there lies a rocky isle,

Where fiery vapour, like the clouds, revolves,

    Then flames, and flings forth rock for many a mile ! "

So HERMANN kindled at the fight ;
   Resolved, like floods of fiery foam,
Over the ice-crown'd Alps to roll his might
   Down on the plains of Rome !—

To die there !—or the Capitol invade,
   And hard by JOVE's high fane demand
Of mad TIBERIUS, and his fathers' shade,
   Right for his plunder'd Fatherland.

Therefore he claim'd the chieftain's rule
   Among the princes : and they slew him then !
He lies in blood, who cherish'd in his soul
   His country more than other men !

DARMOND

O HELA, hast thou heard
   My tears that burning fall ?
'Tis thine to give a just award :
   O HELA, hear their call !

KERDING.

In Walhalla SIGMAR rests beneath the golden ash ;[7]
In his hand the victor's branch ; the lances round him clash.
By TUISCO beckon'd, and by MANA's hand led on,
There the youthful hero-sire receives his youthful son.

WERDOMAR.

But SIGMAR there in silent woe
   His HERMANN greets again.
Not now TIBERIUS and the shades below
   He challenges at JOVE's high fane.

---

[7] *The Golden Ash.*—"'Where,' asked Gangler, 'is the chief or holiest seat of the gods?' 'It is under the ash, Yggdrasill,' replied Har, 'where the gods assemble every day in council . . . . That ash is the greatest and best of all trees. Its branches spread over the whole world, and even reach above heaven.'"—PROSE EDDA.

MY FATHERLAND.

THE boy is silent long
  Through early springs, though words of fire
Would fain tell forth the love so strong
  He bears his silver-hair'd and deed-crown'd sire.

The flame breaks forth at noon of night;
  His bosom glows.
The wings of rosy morning wave in sight,
  He hastens to his sire — but nought his lips disclose.

So was I silent.   Modest shame
  Restrain'd me with stern arm and look;
The light airs rose, and sounds spontaneous came,
  But o'er the lyre my hand, misgiving, shook.

I can forbear no longer : I must take
The lute and lofty utterance learn.
The spell of silence I will break,
And tell the thoughts that in me burn.

Spare me, my Fatherland ! With old renown
Thy brows are wreath'd, immortal thou dost stand.
And lookest proud on many a country down.
Ah ! well I love thee, Fatherland !

Ah ! it is done ! my hand the venture braves,
And trembles down the silver thread !
Spare me, oh, spare ! How bright thy garland waves !
How proud the immortal pathway thou dost tread !

A gentle smile I see,
That fills my heart with full content.
I sing to Echo, joyous, that to me
That gentle smile was sent.

Thine was I from my boyhood. When my breast
Felt the first pulses of ambition spring,
I chose, from heroes of the lance and crest,
HENRY, thy rescuer to sing.

But I beheld that higher track of light,
  And more than mere ambition fired my mind.
The pathway I preferr'd that leads from night
  Up to the Fatherland of all our kind.

That I pursue.   But when the toil too much
  O'erburdens this mortality,
I turn aside, and to the Telyn's touch
  Sing, Fatherland, thy fame to thee.

Round him who brings forth thoughts and deeds sublime
  Thy grove its umbrage casts profound;
It stands and mocks the storm of time,
  And mocks the bush-wood round.

Him whom keen sight and hours propitious bore
  To delve beneath the shadow of thy leaves,
No magic rod that points to golden ore,
  To mines of novel thought, deceives.

From thy young stems the kingdom by the Rhone,
  The forests by the Thames, their saplings took;
And there to other woods are grown
  The offsets of thy parent stock.

Thine are they still.   The iron clank
   Rung from the armour of the warrior-band
By thee sent forth : the Gaul became a Frank,
   England was named from Angle-land.

Yet louder rang thy weapons.   Lofty Rome,
   By the wolf suckled to the pride of war,
Reign'd the world's tyrant.   Thou didst come,
   And leave the wolf-bred weltering in her gore !

Never was land so just as thou
   To others.   Be not over-just.
They are not generous enough to know,
   How in thy fault thou stand'st august !

Simple thou art in manners and in look,
   Earnest, and wise of heart : thy word is strong.
Keen is thy sword ; but to the reaper's hook
   Soon chang'd, nor dripping with the blood of wrong !

Warn'd by that arm of iron, I am still,
   Till she in peace again let fall her hand ;
And muse on thoughts of an exalted will
   Worthy to prove of thee, my Fatherland.

SONG OF FATHERLAND,

WRITTEN FOR JOHANNA ELIZABETH VON WINTHEM.

I AM a German girl :
    Mine eye is blue, and soft its smile.
I have a heart
    Noble and proud, and free from guile.

I am a German girl :
    My blue eye looks on him with scorn,
Him my heart hates
    Who spurns the land where he was born.

I am a German girl :
    No other land I'd choose before
My Fatherland,
    Though I might choose from ev'ry shore.

I am a German girl :

  My lofty look does him deride,

I such a choice,

  Who lingers ere he can decide.

Thou art no German youth :

  Unworthy thou to live and die

In Fatherland,

  Who lov'st it not as well as I.

Thou art no German youth :

  I do disdain thee — heart and soul,

Who Fatherland

  Dishonourest, alien and a fool !

I am a German girl :

  My proud warm heart beneath my hand

Leaps nobly up

  At the sweet name of Fatherland.

So leaps it at the name

  Of that good, noble, German youth

Who Fatherland

  Loves, as I love, with pride and truth.

THE CHIMNEY-CORNER.

" WHEN at first breath of odorous May flowers
       Morn wakes the rosy hours,
From every dewy spray the woods repeat
       Their vocal greeting sweet ;
And he who dwells in woodland huts apart
       Sees thee how fair thou art,
Nature ! and youthfully the old man's eye
       Looks thankful-bright, and nigh
The stripling carols.   Sprightly as the fawn
       He leaps from bush to lawn,
Then climbs the hills that peer above the trees
       And stands to gaze, and sees
The crimson-footed waker of the day
       Over the mountains stray,
And feels the spring in wafted airs of morn
       Around him softly borne.

" When, waking in December's frosty rime,
    Glitters the morning-prime,
The forest songsters greet him, flitting glad
    From sprays with silver clad,
And try by starts, inventive, a new lay
    Stored for the coming May.
Then he who dwells in rural huts apart
    Sees thee how fair thou art,
Nature ! More cheerly looks, and strong,
    The old man ; and the young
Feels more himself, and leaps forth as the roe
    Down to the herd below ;
And to the star-set inland sea he flees,
    And looks around, and sees
The crimson-footed waker of the dawn
    Half into cloud withdrawn.
Soft-gleaming Winter covers vale and hill
    Around him, and is still.
· Oh ! joys of glad December !'—so he spake —
    Nor paused, but trod the lake,
And wing'd his foot with steel. His urban friend
    Thither did early wend

T

From the hearth-side. Far off upon his steed
    He watch'd the landman's speed,
How o'er the crystal plain he onward swung,
    And the ice behind him rung.
' Oh! joys of glad December!'—so he sings;
    The townsman too—and springs
Down from his steed, that stands in vapour dank;
    His mane hangs wet and lank.
Now he fits on the pinions of the skate,
    And breaks his way elate
Through the dry reeds, that springing from below,
    Like arrows of the bow,
Fly to the shore. As afterwards the string
    Does to the arrow ring,
So rings the frost-bound water to the reeds
    Behind him as he speeds.
The feeling of full health and true delight
    Streams from the joyous flight,
And the cool breath of the ethereal flood
    Fans their impetuous blood,
And in the subtlest network of the nerves
    Due equipoise preserves.

Unwearied they the flying dance renew,
  And swing the whole day through.
That musicless delights them.   When at e'en
  The roasted roots have been
Their glad repast, they leave with jocund mirth
  The ashes on the hearth,
And gird their heel to break the still repose,
  That glimmering midnight strows.
They seek the raptures of a bolder race,
  The flying stars they chase,
And him deride, who in the hearth-nook deep
  Cowers, and yawns to sleep.
The sketching artist fain himself would be
  Those forms of health and glee :
Fain would exchange both his rewards and art
  To share their joyous part."

When thus the tender Weakling said his say,
  He closer hugged his clay
And puff'd dull whiffs.   Upon the hearth the fire
  Burnt louder, and burnt higher,

And crack'd and sparkled in the new-piled wood.
Dimmer and denser stood,
Above the full and most immoderate bowl.
Whence fumes of toddy roll,
The punch-cloud.   On the tattlers' studs encrust
Red spots of gnawing rust.

EDONE.

THY lovely form, Edone,
　　Before me flits in air ;
But ah ! mine eye is tearful
　　That Edone is not there !

I see it in the twilight,
　　And when the moon looks fair.
I see it, and am tearful
　　That Edone is not there !

By blossoms I will cull her
　　Down in the vale beneath,
By myrtles I will gather
　　To twine for her a wreath,

I do adjure thee, Phantom,
    Stay, where thou flitt'st in air!
Stay, and transform thee, Phantom
    And be Edone there!

WARNING.

'Gainst Him ye rise,
  Whose mighty Name
The lips of the wise
  Dare scarcely proclaim.

Ye strive with Him,
  Whom in dread amaze
The seraphim
  With the Godhead praise.

On death and on life
  Ye pass your award,
And with Fate at strife
  Ye judge e'en the Lord.

O rebels, in scorn
   Ye blame the Most High
That ye were born,
   And that ye must die.

If unfrenzied ye stand,
   Nor weak as babe led
By the mother's hand,
   Stoop down in dread!

There was one that died
   Who your pathway had trod,
Who had judged in pride,
   And he stood before God.

The beam clank'd aloud,
   His father wept there;
His mother did shroud
   Her face in despair.

The beam did clank, clank;
   His friend turn'd aside;
In sorrow sank
   His departed bride.

The beam that weighs right
  Did fearfully clank :
This scale mounted light,
  And that downward sank.

PREDICTION.

TO COUNT CHRISTIAN AND F. Z. STOLBERG.

THE Telyn rested on the oak. Around
Breathed the light airs : and from it soon there broke
  Spontaneous music. But the sound
  I heard unheeding, nor awoke.

Then made she louder murmur, and her tone
Whirr'd angry forth. I hasten'd to restore
  The concord, lest resentful grown
  She should respond to me no more.

Bards by the war-steed's eyes, and by his prance,
His pawing, snorting, neighing, and his bound,
  Predicted. Mine, too, is the glance
  That penetrates the far profound.

Will the yoke gall for ever ?   O my land,
It yet shall fall.   Pass but one century more !
    'Tis done ! and Reason lifts her wand
    There where the sword-right ruled before.

For in the wood he snorted, and his mane
Flung to the wind ; and with neck proudly borne
    That war-horse did the ground disdain,
    And storm and torrent held in scorn.

He trod the meadow, and did stamp and neigh,
Looking around : then, careless, cropp'd his food :
    Nor to the rider turn'd, who lay
    Hard by the mere-stone in his blood.

The yoke galls not for ever.   Fatherland,
Thou shalt be free !   Pass but one century more !
    'Tis done ! and Reason lifts her wand
    There where the sword-right ruled before.

THE LESSON OF ART.

The springtide, Aëdi, is come ;
    Blue are the heavens, the air is clear.
The west winds breathe of odorous bloom,
    The hour of song, my Aëdi, is here.

" Oh ! no, I cannot sing ;
    My ear is deafen'd with the finch's note ;
Upon the bough I'd rather swing,
    And see my image in the crystal float."

Not sing ? Nor think'st thy mother's heart
    Will chide thy coy delay ?
'Tis spring, and thou must learn thy part.
Full many are the charms of art,
    And few the days of May.

Come from the waving tree,

   And hear what Orphea, queen of nightingales.

Sang to me once of Art's enchanting spell.

   Though my voice trembling fails

Listen, and sing it after me.

   Thus Orphea sang it well:

Now thou must flute it with a stronger sound;

   Now with a lighter, till the tones are lost.

Then warble to the woods around.

Flute, flute it, till in brakes with roses crown'd

   The tones are lost.

" I cannot sing it so: how can I, mother?

   Oh be not angry that I cannot sing!

Sang she no other song — no other —

   The queen of nightingales in spring?

Nothing of that which makes the cheek to glow,

Which makes the cheek turn pale, and tears to flow?"

    Yet more she sang, I wis.

     Oh how it glads me, Aëdi,

    That you have ask'd for this !

     She sang the heart's song tenderly.

Now will I seek thee out the supplest tree,
   And bend the branches low,
That thou thyself may'st nearer see
   In the brook's silver flow.
Thus to the woodland throng
Sang Orphea, queen of song.

The youth stood by and twined a wreath,
   Then dropp'd it with dejected air ;
The maiden quell'd her heart beneath
   Her bosom, and look'd cold and fair.
Then Philomel upon the spray
Sang them a soul-awaking lay.
Towards the youth the maiden drew,
The youth unto the maiden flew :
   They wept for joy that day.

PRINCE-PRAISE.

THANKS to my Genius that from manhood's prime
　　Thou didst resolve, nor from thy vow depart,
Never by adulation of smooth rhyme
　　To desecrate thy holy art:

Never by praise of sots, or glittering flies,
　　Of conquerors, or tyrants without swords,
Of Atheists, that fribble to be wise,
　　Half-men who deem them in dull earnest lords

Of nobler mould than ours.　Not ancient lays,
　　Nor tinsel glimmering with delusive ray,
Nor friends that, dazzled, wonder'd in amaze,
　　Turn'd thee, my Genius, from thy course away.

For thou, in trifles, as a summer shoot
    Art pliant, and dost easily conform ;
But in grave matters, striking deeper root,
    An oak thou standest to the storm.

Though sculptured marble rose above thy sod,
    'Twere but a pillar of thy shame, if rang
Thy lyre with strains that honour'd as a god
    White nigger and ourangoutang.

Not lightly rest, thou idolizer's dust !
    Yours is the fault, that History alone
Can build a monumental bust,
    And Poesy our sons disown.

Yours — that with trembling hand the lyre
    I tuned to Frederic, in Dania's land :
Yours — that to Baden's Frederic the wire
    I touch with trembling hand.

For who is he, the searching friend of truth.
    Who tries the vouchers ?   Go, their witness sift !
Then tax me, if thou canst in sooth,
    With desecration of the poet's gift.

THE MONUMENT.

" YES, thou art Shadow, Friendship, in the sun,
And Shelter when the winter storm blows chill."
So felt we, when our friendly work was done
Upon the pirate's watch-tower hill.[1]

There stand the oaks; and in their shade is set,
Graved with our names, the dear memorial stone.
To him who scrapes the moss, or dares to whet
His axe to fell the tall stems down,—

[1] Stortbeker's, a famous pirate of the Baltic in the pre-
ceding century.

Gräfin Holk, the wives of Cramer and Von Winthem, Graf
Holk, the two Cramers, father and son, and Klopstock, chose
the oaks on this isle to be memorials of their friendly society,
and gave their names respectively to each.

U

Beside whose saplings twice the priestess white
Stood and sang to us, " *Choose no other land*,"
   Till, at the second spell, a gleam of light
      Shew'd where the monument should stand,—

Windema's voice be but a peacock's shriek,
And Tesse's[2] smile a marmoset's grimace!
   Yet why this mild indulgence? why so weak
      My song?   To other sounds give place!

Him let the gozzard 'mid his goslings jeer!
And him, the hero of the hornbook, blithe
   For sport or quarrel! him, with scornful sneer,
      Who whets upon the lawn his scythe!

Knight-starr'd and garter'd, let him win to wife
A housemaid shrew at Hymen's lottery urn;
   And fret and fume through an uneasy life,
      Impatient of a wife's cothurn!

---

[2] *Tesse* was a familiar name given to the daughter Holk, as
an abbreviation of *Comtesse.*

And when he falls one day, soak'd through with rum,
Let him see dimly through the shades rush on
    Stortbeker's ghost, to seize and plunge him dumb
        Into the hissing Phlegethon!

TRANQUILLITY.

Loud from hoar time through all the clefts it rung,
  Through all the labyrinths of Wisdom's laws,
By which she seeks the fount whence all things sprung—
  " Nought is without its cause !"

Nought ?   Is not God, I ween ?
  Then cry they, guided by no certain clue,
" God to himself the cause has been "—
  Their cries it irks me to renew.

He — so we lisp of the Unspeakable—
  Being of Beings, owns no primal source ;
But look above, beneath, around, and tell,
  How causes take from Him their hidden course.

To things created with a living soul
  The secret of their strength — a freeborn will —
Is the Creator's crown-work of the whole,
  That He may mark us meet for good or ill.

        That HE may mark!
          For we of finite mind
          Pass on ourselves so blind
        A judgment dark.

Diverse to spirits is the power of thought,
  They stand on higher, now on lower, grade.
Diverse their freedom : these hath Genius taught
  To soar ; and those stand feeble and afraid.

True freedom is the fount of far resolve,
  Which e'en the Allwise forecasts not in the bud ;
But ever working while the years revolve
  He guides it to the universal good.

      Praise Him who sits not in reflective rest,
      But in perpetual agency is blest,
      And from the fount of our volition leads
      At will the ocean of our moral deeds.

O boundless ocean, how thy waves reply,
  And thunder through all worlds! And when He will
He walks thy billows, who can raise them high
  And lay them still.

  Praise — that my soul is free,
    Praise to the Sire above.
  But what were freedom's self to me
    Could I my God not know, my God not love!

THE WARRIORS.

MARCH, 1778.

THE Braga-song in solitude
   I sang unto myself alone,
Save in the shade my Stolberg stood,
   And listen'd by the mossy stone.
And thus to me the Telyn spoke,
When light I lean'd it on the oak.

Great is the hero of the fight?
   Yes, if he strive in freedom's cause,
Or battle with ensanguin'd Might,
   That clanks her chains o'er trampled laws.
Then is he worthy of his name,
And nobly wins immortal fame.

But if the hero be no more
   Than bloodstain'd conqueror fierce and fell,
Though o'er him loud the trumpets pour,
   And monumental columns tell
His dark and ignominious fate,
Shall he too be accounted great?

And what, then, if he be indeed
   A dwarf'd abortion of the brave?
All impotent in time of need
   His trembling Fatherland to save,
When loud exulting sweeps the plain
Some Attila or Tamerlane?

MY BOSQUET.

TO THE COUNT AND COUNTESS HOLCK.

OLD are your oaks, umbrageous wood!
  And these tall stems that rise sublime
I planted not; but here ye stood
      Before my time.

Still vigorous ye lift your head,
  And lengthen in the day's decline
Your shadows.   Long survive me dead:
      I nought repine!

The rose-briers and the weeping willows
  I plant around; that when the sun
Goes down among the crimson billows
      Some happy one

At eve within thy bower may say,
   " It weeps not, love, it only moans
Soft music. like the willow's play
              Of fabled tones."

When storms no longer rouse the oak,
   Nor willows more their sighs impart,
The songs shall linger still that spoke
              From heart to heart.

THE ACCUSERS.

Iᴛ passes all that stirr'd my blood !
And from its foul and hideous ken
  I scarce escaped the doom
  To hate my fellow men.

A fire that eats into the bones
Is hate to him who feels its sway :
  To him whom it assails,
  A terror and dismay.

To me it was the most abhorr'd
Of every ill my fancy shaped.
  Yet from its loathèd power
  Scarcely my soul escaped.

Ye rage in madness and accuse,
His foresight at your judgment bar;
    Him ye condemn, who set
    Orion's brightest star;

Who Leo, and the lofty Scale,
The Eagle, Altar, and the Urn,
    And in the crown the Rose,
    Bade in their courses burn.

Or else ye cringe, and weak defend
His Providence in doubtful strife,
    Who made the stars to shine
    And peopled them with life.

Weak ye defend, and vain excuse.
By feeble or by foolish cause;
    By things ye fable true,
    Ye vindicate His laws.

Him, before you, I would not name!
The spirit of that sage profound
    Who never but with awe,
    And looks upon the ground,

After deep silence, and with head
Uncover'd, named that holy Name,
    Would rise methinks, and stern
    The profanation blame.[1]

The image of an earnest thought
(Would it were fond delusion!) glows
    Before me; and few doubts
    Its verity oppose.

Shall souls— but turn away your ear! —
Who God accuse, excuse, condemn,
    Live on beyond the grave?
    Is endless life for them?

[1] Robert Boyle.

SEPARATION.

How seriously thou lookest on the bier
    That bore the corpses by!
Fearest thou death?—" Not that I fear."
    What then?—" I fear to die."

I fear not either.—" Then no fear is thine?"
    Alas! I fear, I fear
The mutual pang 'twixt me and mine
    That severs friends so dear

'Twas that which made me with yet sadder breast,
    And with more serious eye,
Look on when to their final rest
    They bore the corpses by.

FALSE PERCEPTION

TO FREDERIC THE GREAT.

Thou who with keenest vision didst discern
The despot's road to immortality,
    But not the many treacherous paths that turn
      To trackless wilds delusively,

Thou sawest not how German art rose high,
From a firm root a lasting stem, and threw
    Deep shadows round. E'en then thou didst deny
      To its fair growth the freshening dew.

Where then, O Frederic, was thine eagle glance
When rose the spirit's might, will, power, and all
    That fostering kings can recompense perchance,
      But cannot into being call?

Be proud, ye bards, that through the wandering maze
Ye saw the steeper path.　Without the dew
　　The oak-wood flourish'd, and new sprouts and sprays
　　　Spring-zephyrs waved and murmur'd through.

Yet might he list to German song, whose ear
Had own'd the witch'ry of Tudescan rhyme,
　　Wherewith he laid the shades of royal care,
　　　And ghosts of fight and sanguine crime !

Thee thy lay saves not from oblivion dark.
Deeds are thy tombstone.　But the poet's meed
　　Is. that Time touches not the master's work,
　　　While History clouds the master's deed.

That cloud is darker, if thou tell the tale
Thyself ; and darker as thou giv'st it sheen.
　　Through chinks of casual candour thou shalt fail
　　　To shed the light of truth serene.

HER DEATH.

(MARIA THERESA.)

SLEEP softly, greatest of thy race.
  Because thou wert most human-hearted !
That truth on graven rocks shall trace
  Hist'ry, who judges the departed.

Oft would I sing of thee.   Elate
  My lyre began with self-toned swell.
I let it sound.   For as they hate
  On all that was not noble fell.

So did I hate, austerely proud,
  E'en to its latest lingering shade,
E'en to its lightest incense-cloud,
  The flattery to princes paid.

x

Now I can sing thee unreprov'd.
  No snake's tongue more will hiss thy praise.
But my faint hand o'er thee beloved
  Along the strings dejected strays.

Yet one assay ! one word of flame.
  And vocal song !   Thy son may strive,
Pant, wrestle, thirst, and weep for fame :
  But can he to thy fame arrive ?

Frederic may bend his hoary head
  Toward the future.   But will she
Who graves on rocks the mighty dead
  Inscribe his destiny with thee ?

Softly, Theresa, sleep !   Thou sleep ?
  Nay, thou dost deeds yet more humane.
Rewarded where men cease to weep
  For all thy sympathies and pain.

MORNING SONG.

(FROM THE SPIRITUAL SONGS.)

WHEN I rise again to life
  From the tranquil sleep of death,
And released from earthly strife
  Breathe that morning's balmy breath.
I shall wake to other thought ;
The race is run, the fight is fought.
All the pilgrim's cares are dreams
When that dawn of morning gleams

Help ! that no departed day,
  God of endless life and joy.
To the righteous Judge may say,
  'Twas profaned by my employ.

To another morn I wake,
And to Thee my offering make.
Oh ! may all my days that flee,
Joys and sorrows, lead to Thee.

Gladly may I see them fled,
    When the twilight o'er me creeps.
When the darkening vale I tread,
    And my friend beside me weeps !
Death assuage, the pang remove.
Let me then the stronger prove.
Vanquishing with heavenward breath.
While I praise thee. Lord of death !

THE RESURRECTION.

(FROM THE SPIRITUAL SONGS.)

YES! thou wilt rise, wilt rise as Jesus rose,
　My dust, from brief repose.
　　Endless to live
　Will He who made thee give.
　　Praise ye the Lord.

Again to bloom the seed the sower sows.
　The Lord of harvest goes
　　Gathering the sheaves,
　Death's sickle reaps and heaves.
　　Praise ye the Lord.

Oh ! day of thankfulness and joyful tears,
  The day when God appears !
    When 'neath the sod
    I have slept long, my God
      Will wake me up.

Then shall we be like unto them that dream,
  And into joy supreme
    With Jesus go.
    The pilgrim then shall know
      Sorrow no more.

Ah ! then my Saviour me shall lead in grace
  To the Most Holy Place,
    If Him I serve
    This side the veil, nor swerve.
      Praise ye the Lord.

THE END.